D0355985

Presented To:

_____

From:

_____

Date:

_____

an APPLE *for* the ROAD

an APPLE *for* the ROAD

❖

Wisdom for Life

Compiled by Pam Spinosi

Photos by Noémie Fabreguette

DESTINY IMAGE® PUBLISHERS, INC.

P.O. Box 310, Shippensburg, PA 17257-0310

"Promoting Inspired Lives."

This book and all other Destiny Image, Revival Press, MercyPlace, Fresh Bread, Destiny Image Fiction, and Treasure House books are available at Christian bookstores and distributors worldwide.

For a U.S. bookstore nearest you, call 1-800-722-6774.

For more information on foreign distributors, call 717-532-3040.

Reach us on the Internet: www.destinyimage.com.

ISBN 10: 0-7684-4133-1   ISBN 13: 978-0-7684-4133-8

Ebook ISBN: 978-0-7684-8828-9

For Worldwide Distribution, Printed in the U.S.A.

1 2 3 4 5 6 7 8 9 10 11 / 13 12

DEDICATION

This book is dedicated to the students of Bethel School of Supernatural Ministry, who bring so much joy to our church and our city and then go out to change the world.

Endorsements

An Apple for the Road is a compilation of stories from several of our Bethel Church staff. I thought I knew them quite well; after all, I hired most of them. But as I read their stories, hidden treasures began to emerge from the pages of this book. Their honesty and transparency so moved me that I was literally undone inside. The courage it took to uncover their dreams, fears, and failures is inspiring as well as convicting. Their testimonies will challenge you to press into God for greater manifestations of His very presence.

To be honest, I've read a hundred manuscripts and heard thousands of testimonies, and they always encourage me. But this manuscript reads like the book of Acts; you can feel the authenticity of each author as you peer behind the veil of their intimate relationship with Jesus.

An Apple for the Road is like watching a great love story unfold or reading a well-written romance novel. No matter who you are, this book will make you hungry for deeper encounters with God. I think *every* believer should read this book!

Kris Vallotton
Co-Founder of
Bethel School of Supernatural Ministry

Author of seven books including,
The Supernatural Ways of Royalty

Senior Associate Leader of
Bethel Church, Redding, California

A word fitly spoken is like apples of gold in settings of silver. —Proverbs 25:11

Contents

PART 2.
LOVING OTHERS

PART 3.
LIVING LIFE

PREFACE

To Bethel School of Supernatural Ministry, thousands of students have come to fan the flames of their passion for God, receive instruction and impartation, and grow in moving in the supernatural in order to see God's kingdom spread through all the earth in every realm of societal influence. Many of them stay for three years and leave equipped to see the impossible bow the knee to the Lord Jesus as they preach, prophesy, heal the sick in the name of Jesus, and follow the leading of the Holy Spirit to invade the dark places of the earth with the glory of God.

In the third-year deployment program, interns work under various leaders at Bethel, who mentor them in the areas of the interns' interest.

Two years ago, I had interns, so I could attend the monthly meetings for them at which a Bethel senior leader would share and host a Q & A session. As I listened to their questions, many of which seemed to be about practical things of life, I got the idea for this book: life lessons from Bethel leaders.

Several people came immediately to mind because of certain life messages they carried that I felt were pertinent. Others seemed to be highlighted to me. While there is an enormous pool of wisdom to draw from at Bethel Church, and I would have liked to include chapters from about 40 others, I have assembled a small group of mostly previously unpublished writers who have much to say and from whom I suspect we will hear much more in days to come. (Look for their full-length books in the very near future.) Each one is special:

Joaquin Evans is co-leader of Bethel Movement Activation Teams; previously, he was the Healing Rooms director. His sensitivity to the Holy Spirit is so beautiful. Joaquin's spiritual radar can recognize His voice no matter whom He is speaking through. His love for the Holy Spirit spills out on everyone around him, refreshing them and enabling them to run after the *more*. His heart for God comes out in everything he does.

When I asked Chris Gore, current Healing Rooms director, to write a chapter, I hoped he would choose the topic he chose. Every time I hear him share it, I weep. I am greatly touched by the testimonies of his ministry.

I so appreciate Deborah Stevens, our events director, not only for the excellence with which she does her work, but also for the depths of her hunger for God, love for others, and capacity for joy. She's a truly great person.

A few months ago, I was in a meeting at which a BSSM pastor, Sheri Downs, led worship. It was one of those moments when the worship leader was so in tune with the Lord that others could encounter Him powerfully, too. At least that was how it was for me. I really heard Him call me as she sang. Such is the preciousness of her walk with Him.

I love Stefanie Overstreet's story of her romance with our outreach pastor, Chris. I've been waiting for years for her and Chris to come out with the book about it! So to prod things along a bit, and because I felt others would be blessed by her story, I invited her to contribute.

I've always been impressed with Global Legacy director, Paul Manwaring's, story about how God called him and led him in interesting paths. What he has to say is so important for all those grappling with the questions of what to do with their lives and what "ministry" looks like for them. I am so pleased he was willing to share his story in this book.

Though I don't know Crystal Stiles, another BSSM pastor, well, I felt led to ask her to contribute. I've appreciated her heart for prayer, and just recently I heard her receive a prophetic word that showed how God sees her. It's a time of promotion for her. Yea, Crystal.

I'm grateful to our senior leader, Bill Johnson, whose words, life, and writings inspire us all and who permitted me to assemble notes from some of his messages to the interns as a concluding chapter for this book. I first got the idea for this book while listening to him share insights from a rich and very fruitful life with God.

And now, here's a glimpse of lessons forged in life by some who *write that others may run.*

Pam Spinosi
Redding, California

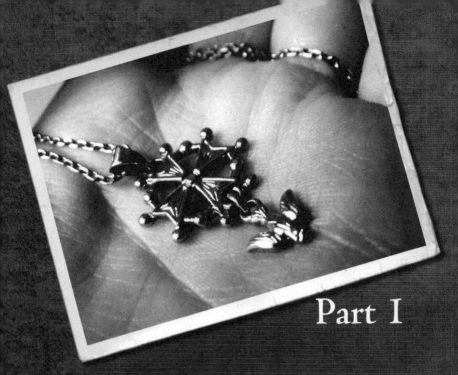

Part I

LOVING GOD

This is a photo of a Huguenot cross. The Huguenots —16th century French Protestants— experienced great miracles and visitations from God, but endured intense persecution from their countrymen. Hundreds were martyred, and many eventually fled to neighboring countries as well as far-off lands like the United States and South Africa, where their character and expertise in many fields made them a great blessing. This cross represents a people so stalwart in their faith and alive in their relationship with God that they persevered in the face of harsh opposition. Their legacy endures, and their intimacy with God created some of the rich wells of revival from which the French may draw for ages to come.

Chapter I

Holy Spirit, My Best Friend

by Joaquin Evans

I have a best friend,
and His name is Holy Spirit!

It was late afternoon in Jerusalem, and I was preparing to speak at the first OneThing conference in Israel. There were about 1500 people in attendance, from youth to adults, and this would be my first time speaking while an event was being televised live internationally. I was so excited to be a part of such a monumental event, but to say I was a little bit nervous would have been an understatement. The other speakers were international headliners, and then there was me. Gulp. Good thing God is in a good mood!

My assignment was simply to activate the young people in attendance in supernatural ministry and evangelism. No big deal, right? In addition to the bit of pressure I was already feeling, I was meant to do this in only two sessions of 50 minutes each, including the teaching and ministry time. Fifty minutes may sound like a lot of time unless you are trying to shift the mindsets of a group of individuals who are a part of an admittedly stubborn culture, are in constant threat of war, and have never been exposed to the miraculous before. Preachers will tell you it takes 15 minutes just to say "hello." On top of all this, there was a small taped off square section on the floor for the speakers to stand in so the cameras could capture them. If I stepped out of the square, some cameraman would be in my face waving me back. Can you feel my pressure mounting?

As my speaking slot was approaching, I was not feeling very confident in my ability to make the type of impact I needed to in such a short period of time. I wasn't sure what I was going to say or how I was going to fit it all in, but what I did know was that three times that day, while praying into the event, I could literally feel the person of Holy Spirit come and stand just behind my left shoulder. Wow. What an amazing experience!

In my nervousness, I was not hearing any great revelation, and I can't say I got a download of everything that needed to happen, but He was there! The One I love, my friend, Holy Spirit, was there. I did not feel Him in that way the whole day, but just those few distinct times when He made Himself overtly known, letting me know He was there.

I want to say that His presence made me feel supremely confident. It didn't, but it did help. In the early parts of the session, I could feel the apprehension of those who were hearing this part of the Good News for the first time. Could they really believe the things I was saying, and could God really be that good to them and through them? As the session went on, I could feel their mindsets shifting and their expectancy starting to rise. Near the end of the session, they were starting to open to His goodness. Faith was rising! In response, God's presence was starting to come in the room. My friend, Holy Spirit, was finding a place to rest. Our hearts are His resting place, and everywhere there are surrendered hearts, hearts in alignment with His reality, which is His goodness, those hearts have access to Him. And maybe even more importantly, He has access to them.

I did not want to lose the momentum that was building, and I knew I had another short session the next day, so I preached right up until nearly the final moment when they were soon going to shut the cameras off and the session would be over. My intention was to release as much truth as I could at that time and go after the demonstration of His supernatural goodness the next day.

With only a minute left, I asked everyone who was truly hungry for the things I had been sharing to please stand up. I was going to pray a quick corporate impartation over the group and come back ready to go the next day. When I started to pray, however, I felt my friend come and stand just behind my left shoulder again. Holy Spirit was there, and He was so jealous for the affection of the ones He loves that He could not wait another day. As I prayed my impartation prayer, a word of knowledge for healing dropped into my spirit. I knew our time was done, so I wrestled if I should give it or not, but I decided to let that one out, and as I announced it, another came, then another. And then something truly amazing happened.

A young lady sitting on the front row, who had fallen and broken her ankle during worship the night before and had been carried out of the service in the sight of everyone, stood up. Holy Spirit, with His own agenda, had told her to stand on her ankle, which was in an air-cast. When she did, there was no pain. He then told her to jump on it, which she did, with no pain. He then told her to dance, so she ripped off the cast and started jumping and dancing along the front. As the people saw the girl, who they knew was in an air-cast from her injury from the night before, dancing up at the front of the stage, miracles began to break out through the crowd. I called for those who had just been healed to come forward, and the people started to stream to the front. At that point, the camera director was signaling me to keep going because they did not want to miss a minute of what was happening. Many, many people were healed that day, some of deafness, some from arthritis, and some of pain from accidents from over 20 years ago. A young lady who is now a co-leader for our Healing Rooms dance ministry was healed of a chronic neck condition in that meeting. Wow, how I love Holy Spirit and His presence!

The Idea of God or the Person of God

For way too long, we have traded the person of God for the idea of God. We settle for concepts and theories instead of encounters and the presence, the Person. Why? God made Himself available. Why should we make Him unavailable? There is a burning and longing in His heart to know us personally, yet we have bought into the lie that knowing about Him is the highest standard. Knowing about Him is not *Him*. He is jealous for His Bride. Finding Him is easier than we ever thought. The first step is knowing that we can.

Belief or Faith

My life was completely and radically changed the day Jesus released the presence of His beloved Holy Spirit into my life. The Church is in a beautiful process of learning to simply live what it believes. Much of the Church believes things that they never see or experience. Why? Because in order for belief to move into faith, it needs to have expectancy connected to it. Faith is the muscle that moves heaven. Take healing, for example. Some people in the Church who genuinely love Jesus do not believe that God heals at all today. They obviously have no belief for this area in their lives. That's OK, because it's the kindness of God that leads people to repentance. But much of the Church believes that God *can* heal; they just never see it happen. It's because they literally have no expectancy for what they believe. This is understandable for those who have never seen or experienced healing themselves. Then there are those who are poised to change the world through His goodness because they have cultivated a heart of genuine expectancy for the things they believe. In other words, they have learned how to put a demand on the anointing. Holy Spirit is the courier of heaven and the primary releaser of the anointing.

Peter demonstrated this lesson in Acts when they were being threatened by the government system of their day and told not to preach Jesus anymore or they would pay a more severe consequence. Peter responded by putting a demand on the anointing. Even before Peter uttered His famous prayer, he expected that it would be answered in some profound way, or under the circumstances he would not have prayed such a bold prayer. He may not have known exactly how it was going to be answered, but he knew God would somehow respond powerfully. In response to their threats, he prayed:

> *"Now, Lord, look on their threats, and grant to Your servants that with all boldness they may speak Your word, by stretching out Your*

hand to heal, and that signs and wonders may be done through the name of Your holy Servant Jesus." And when they had prayed, the place where they were assembled together was shaken; and they were all filled with the Holy Spirit, and they spoke the word of God with boldness (Acts 4:29-31).

I think Peter meant his prayer! Belief aligns us, expectancy connects us, and faith moves heaven and earth.

The Role of Holy Spirit

The amazing news is that Holy Spirit is the one who leads us into *all* truth. (See John 16:13.) Peter prayed to Jesus, but Jesus answered his prayer by sending the Holy Spirit! And He is the One who filled them and allowed them to speak the word with boldness. What a beautiful union. For too long, the Holy Spirit has been an abstract thought in the believer's mind and not a real, loving, tangible person of the Godhead.

I would even suggest that, for most believers, whether they are willing to admit it or not, Holy Spirit has been of less importance than the Father or the Son. It makes perfect sense to me that we cannot expect to walk in the fullness God has for us while only fellowshipping with two-thirds of the Godhead. We know in our minds that all three expressions of God are of equal importance, but what do our hearts tell us, and how do we live our lives? Is Holy Spirit our friend? The simple truth is that no one comes into the kingdom except through Jesus Christ. That is the good news that has set us all free, but Holy Spirit is the expression of God that is assigned to actively lead, guide, and interact with the believer today.

Jesus tells the disciples who have walked with Him for three years and witnessed all His miraculous signs that it is better for them that He go away. What could be better than walking with Jesus on the earth for three solid years and seeing all the amazing things He did for the people He loves? According to Jesus, what is better is making friends with Holy Spirit and having those same miraculous things happen through us!

> *Nevertheless I tell you the truth. It is to your advantage that I go away; for if I do not go away, the Helper will not come to you; but if I depart, I will send Him to you* (John 16:7).

Earlier in John, Jesus specifically tells us that the helper He will send is Holy Spirit. *"But the Helper, the Holy Spirit, whom the Father will send in My name, He will teach you all things, and bring to your remembrance all things that I said to you"* (John 14:26).

John 15:26 even says that the helper, Holy Spirit, will testify of Jesus through us. In Acts 2, Peter declares to the multitude that Jesus was attested to them by miracles, signs and wonders, which he did in their sight. Just like He did for Peter, when Holy Spirit comes upon us and we develop a friendship with Him, He will testify of Jesus through us with miracles, signs, and wonders. What amazingly good news!

Miracles Are Normal in His Presence

I can't say I am particularly good at my job, but Holy Spirit is exceptionally good at His. Miracles have become such a normal part of my life that it is hard to imagine a week without them, a really staggering thought for a guy who was living a "normal" life just over a decade ago. It is normal for miracles to happen on the streets, in church services, and every week in the Healing Rooms. It is normal for deaf ears to open, tumors to dissolve, and even for metal to disappear! The miracles are simply an expression of His goodness released through His presence. As I become better friends with the person of Holy Spirit, He comes more, and as a result, more good things happen. It's impossible to have His presence come and not have good things happen. Truly, it is *"not by might nor by power, but by My Spirit, says the Lord of hosts"* (Zech. 4:6).

Hebrews 11:1 reads, *"Faith is the substance of things hoped for, the evidence of things not yet seen."* Let's look at that! Faith is a *substance*. That means it can be a detectable, tangible reality! His presence is the *substance* of heaven. It's our awareness of His superior reality that allows us dominion in this inferior reality. When His presence comes, we are aware of something greater than ourselves. That awareness is the evidence of things we are about to see. It's the evidence of His realm invading and superseding this inferior realm. Our awareness of Him inherently and instantly increases our expectation for His nature to reign supreme in any situation. It is impossible to become more aware of God and not believe Him more. The two go so hand-in-hand that His presence literally becomes the evidence of the things about to be seen or manifested.

I tell people that when they are praying for an increase in their ability to heal the sick, if they can become aware of His presence in the process, that presence is the evidence of what is available or about to happen. Jesus is not just the Healer; He *is* healing. Where Jesus is, there is no sickness, pain, or disease, so we can say that Jesus is healing. Whenever we can become aware of His presence, healing is available as the automatic by-product. Holy Spirit is the one who teaches us how to be increasingly aware of His presence. When we are aware of His presence, that presence is the evidence of what is about to happen: tumors dissolving, deaf ears opening, arthritis leaving, and more. It becomes simple when we are aware of the One who *is* healing.

Notice I've used the word *aware,* and not *feel,* for recognizing His presence. This is because some people don't feel as much as others, but the goal is to simply be aware, and everyone can do that.

Knowing Him More

My life was for the most part average until I encountered God and, more specifically, the person of Holy Spirit. The presence of God was the fulfillment of my desires long before I knew it. I was happy, my life was pretty good, but it wasn't extraordinary, and it definitely was not supernatural before Him. Jesus didn't just save me; He transformed me into a new creation by the infilling of His Spirit. Some people are hesitant to focus on or pursue Holy Spirit because they feel they can get off track or lose focus on Jesus. Remember, Holy Spirit is the one who leads us into all truth and testifies of Jesus when He comes (see John 16:12-15). What can be safer than that? Let's look at His name. He is the Spirit of *Holiness.* How can the pursuit of a relationship with the one who leads us into all truth, who testifies of Jesus, and who is Himself holy, lead us astray. The Church owes Him much more love and attention than we have given Him.

My full story of getting to know Holy Spirit as a person, as amazing as it is, is too lengthy to include in its entirety in this chapter, but I would like to tell you one of my favorite parts.

During a meeting several years ago, Heidi Baker spoke of knowing Holy Spirit and ministering in the presence of God. This was all brand new to me at the time, but I was so hungry for more. At the end, she prayed a corporate prayer of impartation over the crowd. As she prayed and I hungered in my spirit, I wish I could say I encountered God like a lightning bolt. I didn't. What did happen was that the tips of three of my fingers on my left hand started to go numb, kind of like an icy-hot sensation. Nothing more, except when I put that hand on my friend next to me, he fell over in the presence. That had never happened to me before. Now I was starting to have fun! I laid my hands on my friend standing on the other side of me, and she fell over, too, though not as fast. It was more like the sensation of His presence slowly overcame her. I did not know what exactly was happening, but I could tell it was good!

After that meeting, instead of chalking it up as a good night, going out to dinner, and essentially letting the experience pass by without changing me, I went home and got alone in the den. Inside, I lay on the floor and with a level of astonishment, allowed myself to realize that the God of all creation was touching my fingers! As I let that thought grow, the feeling slowly began to increase and cover my whole hand and then slowly move down my arm. That night I stayed in the den for an hour, maybe more, and His presence covered my whole arm and half my chest.

The next day, I felt great and so much closer to God, but as I went about my day, that feeling of His physical presence was not there like it had been the night before. I was hungry for that amazing experience again so that night I got alone in the den once more and just began to thank God for what I had experienced the night before. As I gave thanks and tried, as vividly as possible, to remember just how that wonderful sensation felt, something amazing happened! The physical, tangible presence came back. First, on my fingertips and then slowly growing to cover my hand, arm, and upper body. This time, it somehow seemed to come a little easier, and it seemed to move over my body a little more quickly.

I would several years later hear Bill Johnson teach that whatever we give thanks for in the kingdom increases. I was finding that to be so true with His presence. And why not? Before we loved Him, He first loved us! The increase did not stop there. Almost every night for the next few weeks, I would lie on the floor and remember with a thankful heart the experience God was sharing with me through His beloved Holy Spirit. What took over an hour the first night began to happen more and more quickly, and the presence would cover more of my body. This most amazing experience was becoming more than a touch; it was becoming a relationship. In those weeks, the presence grew to the point that as soon as I would lie on the floor and begin to give thanks, Holy Spirit would come and rest on me, and it was not just on my fingers or hand, but I was feeling Him on my whole body. I could even feel Him down into my feet! The intensity of His presence also increased, from a lightly warm tingling sensation, the icy-hot feel, to waves or currents, something like low levels of electricity moving through my body. The presence would also often feel very heavy. I have later come to learn that the Bible describes this as the *Kabad* or "the weighty presence of God."

With time, my relationship with Holy Spirit grew to the place that His presence would come as I simply turned the affection of my heart toward Him. He would flood my body, and His presence would cover me. As our relationship increased, I found some of the endearing moments came when I was not focused on Him at all. I could be working or driving in the car and thinking about or doing something totally unrelated to Holy Spirit, but His presence would come flowing over me just as sweetly as if I were worshiping in my den. The first few times it startled me a little, and I did not understand what I had done to cause Him to come. As I inquired with Him about it, He showed me that it is an attribute of true friendship. Sometimes He just wants to be with me! He is so loving.

At Bethel, we live in a culture of honor, and along with the presence, honor is the backbone of sustained revival. True honor is recognizing the greatness that God has put inside of others and treating them accordingly, often even before they recognize that greatness inside of themselves. When the relational foundations of a community are based on honor, those relationships flourish. Honor releases life. It causes people to blossom and become the best version of themselves. Even with all the profound impact I've seen honor have on individuals, I have never seen anyone respond to honor given as quickly or profoundly as Holy Spirit. The moment we turn the attention of our hearts toward Him and even begin to recognize His greatness, His love, or His role as *Parakletos,* helpmate to the Bride, He comes!

Our Destiny in Him

Why are we alive? The Bride—the Church—is corporately waking up to Her destiny in Him, and we, too, as individuals will find our greatest calling in friendship with Holy Spirit. I have a great friend who says, "You are the greatest version of yourself in the anointing." Why? Because the anointing moves us past ourselves and into the person God sees us as. We are bolder, freer, more creative, and more loving in the anointing. These are all things the Father intends for us to live in all the time. It comes back to honor. And God sharing His Spirit with us is one of the most profound ways He shows honor to those who have chosen life through His Son, Jesus.

God is powerfully moving through the nations, and He is preparing to increase that move through the ones who are no longer satisfied with just the idea of God, but instead grasp again the person of God. The Father and Son are both cheering on our part-nership with Holy Spirit as they are, in fact, the ones who ordained it to work this way. In His presence, we will not only find the God-intended version of ourselves, but we will find ourselves operating and loving in ways that change the world around us. We will enter the company of those who are re-writing history and covering the earth with the knowledge of His glory. We will find ourselves as revivalists! For the kingdom of heaven is righteousness, peace, and joy in the Holy Spirit.

If you don't know Holy Spirit, Jesus and the Father desire that you do. If you do know Him, spend time growing your friendship with Him until He consumes you and the kingdom of heaven is moving through you. Spend time each day honoring Him with the affection of your heart, and allow Him to honor you with His presence. A friendship with Holy Spirit will change not only you, but it will also change everything you touch and do into the version God intended for you from the beginning. I bless you as you find more of yourself in more of Him.

Chapter 2

NO OFFENSE TAKEN
by Chris Gore

My journey came to a decision point while I was on a ministry trip in southern India. I had gone to India to participate in a healing crusade with Randy Clark. It was a warm Sunday in January 2006, and I felt that I had heard the Lord say that He wanted to do something special in the lives of children. The day started, and I had the opportunity to preach at a friend's church on the Sunday morning before the evening crusade. I arrived at the church to find that all the children had already been sent home as they had had a children's service earlier in the morning. I thought that somehow I had missed the Lord's voice, so I proceeded with the service. My translator had not shown up, so they asked me to share for 90 minutes until he arrived and then to preach for another 90 minutes once he arrived.

I remember the day so clearly. I preached on my favorite subject, the goodness of God and the reality that our circumstances do not dictate the goodness of God. The preaching time was over, and God's goodness was poured out like water on a parched land. I have found that God can't help but show up when the declaration of His goodness is made. The miracles that happened that morning were simply staggering.

The blind, the deaf, and the lame were healed. We were handed a young baby that was covered in lesions all over her body from head to toe. They were deep and nasty. Right in front of our eyes, the lesions began to dry up, and new skin began to form. We received word the next day from the mother that the baby woke up the next morning with entirely new skin, head to toe. Children began to emerge from everywhere, and the healings flowed.

Another young boy, about 13 years old, had intestinal issues. He received prayer and hit the ground under the power of God. He was out for about 20 minutes, and when he came around, he sat up and asked, "Who was the man that came and took my stomach out, cleaned it, turned it around and put it back in?" That young boy left the service that day pain free. There were many other miracles that morning, and in that church of 225 people, we counted 157 miracles. It was a great day in the kingdom!

We had lunch and returned to our hotel with just enough time to change our shirts and jump onto the bus to head to the crusade, where thousands of hungry people were waiting. What I thought was a fulfillment of what the Lord had spoken to me about was only the beginning. What happened next literally shook me, and I still, to this day, feel the emotion of it as I write. This was the last night of our crusade. The message was completed, and the ministry team was set loose to release the kingdom on the sick and the dying. We as a team had raised $100,000 to hire trucks to go into the surrounding areas up to 30 miles away to bring many sick, dying, deaf, blind, and crippled people to the meetings.

On no other night of the eight crusade nights had this happened, but as I walked through the crowd, a young baby just literally ended up in my arms, almost thrown over the security barrier. The child was healed and passed back. One child after the other was passed over. Some parents wanted blessing and others needed healing, and Jesus healed every one of them. An older lady about 10 deep in the crowd caught my attention. She was holding a young boy, who I later found out was 5 years old. He was asleep in his grandmother's arms.

I asked if I could take him and hold him. "Does he need blessing or healing?" I asked. The grandmother replied, "My grandson has never stood, never taken a step, and never walked in his life." About this time, the boy woke up and burst into tears, as he had a very white man looking down on him, but when he had gone to sleep, he was in a precious Indian lady's arms. I quickly pulled every trick I knew, and the one that settled him down was M&M's and chocolate. The crowd had breached the security barrier and was pushing in around me for my attention, wanting prayer. I was so moved with compassion for the boy, it seemed like he and I were the only people standing in that field that evening. I took him and my friend, Carey, to the front, away from the demands of the crowd.

The little boy was now my friend. (His name in English, I later found out, is translated "bright and shining light.") I told him that my friend Jesus loved him and wanted to heal him. While Carey was making friends with him, I was lying in the dry and dusty soccer field so moved by compassion, and I heard the clear voice of the Lord say, "Pick him up and walk him."

I turned to Carey and told him what I had heard the Lord say, and he said, "I heard exactly the same."

I said, "Let's not think about it, but just be obedient to what we both heard."

We had taught the little boy in his own language to say, "More, Jesus." We told him we were going to walk him, and we just wanted him to say, "More, Jesus." Carey took his torso, and I took his legs, and we began to walk him. To my shock, with Carey holding his torso, he just walked off saying, "More Jesus." We went to holding his arms and then his hands and then his little fingers. I turned to his grandmother, thinking I must have misunderstood, and she was weeping on the ground.

I said, "Did I misunderstand the situation?"

She said, "I already told you. He's never stood, never taken a step, and never walked." It was now past midnight. The truck that the boy came in was due to leave, and he was paged over the PA to return to his truck.

The field was almost empty, and I returned to my bus ready for the hotel. I sat in the bus, overwhelmed with joy by what had just happened, and I heard the Lord say, "Celebrate by getting back on the front line." So I jumped out of the bus, ran back to the soccer field, and found a young lady who had not received prayer and was 100 percent deaf in one ear. I had hardly lifted my hand to her ear, and it popped open.

We returned to the hotel, and I asked Randy why I prayed for 20 minutes for a crippled boy, and he was healed, yet I had prayed for my own daughter's situation for eight years, at that point, and had not seen breakthrough. God began to reveal to me that I was carrying an offense with God that needed to be dealt with. Here is my own story.

My first daughter, Charlotte, was born in 1995. Within a few hours of her birth, she had a massive grand mal seizure. She was in intensive care for three weeks, and when she was about to be sent home, the neurologist took us into her office and said that Charlotte's brain was so damaged that, medically speaking, she would never walk or function in a normal manner. The best thing that we could do for her would be to take her into a loving home environment and love her the very best that we could.

Our journey began, which I believe to this day propelled me into a healing ministry, but I needed to deal with the intellectual offense that was formed toward God. Too many times we hold on to disappointments and burdens, and we wonder why we struggle to walk in a life of fruitfulness.

Dealing with Today's Disappointments; Determining Tomorrow's Fruit

Over the next few years, Charlotte developed scoliosis in her spine, and in 2008, it needed urgent surgery. It twisted to 104 degrees and had affected one side of her lung. Without a miracle or breakthrough, the crushing of her heart would be only a matter of time.

In June 2008, Charlotte underwent one of the most painful operations that a person can have. She needed to have her spine fused from the base of her neck to her tailbone. The operation took eight hours, during part of which she was hung upside down, which resulted in her eyes being swollen shut for almost a week. During the operation, Charlotte lost all her blood five times over and continued to bleed postoperatively for a couple of days. The doctors were at a bit of a loss, and she was monitored closely in intensive care for five days. One morning I walked into her room, closed the glass doors and the curtains, and started to play worship, and I worshiped right in the face of the enemy.

That day I stood there and said, "Regardless of what happens, whether Charlotte makes it through this or not, I will always declare, God, that You are good. I refuse to be offended at You, for this condition is not from You." I made a commitment to God that day that, whenever I preached, I would always declare the goodness of the Lord. I worshiped with all my heart, not to get God to do something, because He has already done it.

Let's not push what is possible into tomorrow because we may not have seen a breakthrough yet. When we do this, we end up creating a theology that *His timing* will be when the miracle happens. But the miracle was paid for over 2000 years ago. His timing for our miracles is *now*. "Today is a great day for a miracle." I have learned to rest in the finished work of the cross, knowing that it's not my works that will bring the manifestation of the miracle.

God's Goodness Is Not Based Upon Our Circumstances

Many times people think that God allows sickness upon them to teach them lessons. They then come to the conclusion that God's heart is different than Jesus' heart and, therefore, that God is warring with Jesus. While they may know that Jesus heals all their diseases, they have this mentality that God allows them to be sick. They know Jesus wants them made whole, but somehow they think that this is not God's heart for them. When we hold to this theology, we create powerless Christianity, and then we wonder why the Church has walked in such defeat. The heart of the Father for His children is that we would walk in wholeness and blessings and receive all that Jesus paid for.

> *Who being the brightness of His glory, and the express image of His person, and upholding all things by the word of His power, when He had by Himself purged our sins, sat down on the right hand of the Majesty on high* (Hebrews 1:3 KJV).

The phrase *express image* is translated from a Greek work that speaks of an identical copy or a perfect representation. Therefore, God's Word reveals that Jesus Christ is the identical copy and perfect representation of His Father. Thus, we can always be confident in determining God's will concerning healing by looking at the life of Jesus.

The Gospels contain not one example of Jesus putting sickness on anybody. Believing that God's heart is not the same as the heart of Jesus is completely contrary to the perfect representation of Christ. He does not give sickness, and it's always His will to heal *all*. That's the good news of the Gospel! Healing is in His nature; it's His name: "Jehovah Rapha."

As Kris Vallotton once said, "I am going to put a chair in front of me, and devil, you are going to sit in it and watch me worship." Within about two hours of me pouring my heart out in worship to God, the doctors came in to check Charlotte and confirmed that the bleeding had stopped and all the tubes could be removed.

I refuse to be offended at God. Not dealing with our disappointments and carrying burdens that were never meant for us will lead to the development of an intellectual offense with God. When I ask a crowd of people, "Is there anyone here who has not had some level of unexplained loss in your life?" I have not yet had a person respond. We have all had unexplained loss in our lives, but it is how we deal with these that will determine the fruit that we walk in tomorrow.

I am reminded of the story in Matthew 14, when Jesus found out that John the Baptist had been beheaded. Scripture tells us that Jesus went to the mountain to be alone with the Father, but never made it as the crowds pushed in needing healing. He healed the sick, walked on water, and had Peter walk on water. The crowds pushed in again for healing, and He healed their sick, then finally removed Himself from the crowd to be alone with the Father.

What was Jesus doing with the Father? I would like to propose several things. Firstly, we need to understand the goodness of the Father. As I explained earlier out of Hebrews 1:3, Jesus is the exact representation of the Father. So I believe Jesus was with the Father to remind Himself of the goodness of His Father. It's out of that place that we are able to minister with power and without limits hanging over our heads regarding whether it is the Father's will to heal or not or whether He is really good or not.

Secondly, if we are going to carry burdens and responsibilities, it will only be a matter of time before the burdens on our backs are too heavy to carry, and in that place, we won't want to pray for anybody else. The good news is that the burden was never meant for us.

His Burden Is Light; His Yoke Is Easy

My favorite miracle in the Bible is the story found in Acts 3:4 of the crippled man at the gate beautiful: *"And fixing his eyes on him, with John, Peter said 'Look at us.'"* I have many messages that have come from this amazing miracle.

The first thing that Peter and John said to the man at the gate beautiful was not, *"Silver and gold have I none."* It was, *"Look at us."* They carried an incredible confidence in the goodness of the Father. I am not referring to self-confidence. I am referring to an unshakable confidence in the goodness and grace of Jesus. They knew who they were, and they knew what they had to give away.

Then they said, *"Silver and gold I do not have, but what I do have I give you..."* (Acts 3:6). We, as believers, are carrying the kingdom, but we can only give away what we know we have. We have to carry an unshakable confidence in the goodness of the Father, knowing that it's always His will to heal. I am not prepared to settle for anything short of the authentic Gospel that we saw Jesus demonstrate. *"The kingdom of God does not come with observation; nor will they say, see here! or see there! For indeed the kingdom of God is within you"* (Luke 17:20-21).

We see an amazing contrast here in Acts 3. First, we see Peter and John saying, *"Look at us"* in verse 4. Then in verse 12, when they come under fire from the religious people of the day, Peter and John say to these men, *"...Why look so intently at us, as though by our own power or godliness we had made this man walk?"* If it's not our glory to take when the miracle happens, why do we take the burden upon ourselves when it does not? I believe that if we take the burden, we will end up taking the glory.

After I do a miracle meeting, one of the first things that I like to do when I return to my hotel is to get with Jesus and say, "Jesus, I have something here that was never meant for me. I take the burden for the people who were not healed tonight, and I leave it at the foot of the cross." And then I say, "Jesus, I also give You any glory that was given to me when it was meant for You."

This leaves me in a place of freedom to walk without burden and without taking the glory. It leaves me in the place of freedom to minister out of the track record of Jesus and not out of my own track record. See, Jesus healed all who came to Him; He's my role model.

It's not in a roulette way that some get healed and some don't—which would imply that if they don't get healed, it does not matter. No, I cannot find one place in Scripture where Jesus addressed unanswered prayer. He walked in an unlimited certainty that prayer is always answered. Jesus is my role model. He healed all those who came to Him.

God does not make a choice to heal some and not others. The choice was made before the foundations of the world, and that choice was paid for in full 2,000 years ago with the stripes that His Son took upon Himself. Yet often we come to the conclusion healing is not God's will because we have not seen a result. By doing this, we have just undermined the standard of the Bible below our personal experience and set a standard that is not biblical. I must live by the standard that Jesus set, and He healed all those who came to Him. I am the one who needs to work out how to have the power of God flowing through me, and that happens by the renewing of my mind. Jesus said:

The thief does not come except to steal, and to kill, and to destroy. I have come that they may have life, and that they may have it more abundantly (John 10:10).

There is one other thing that I do when I bring the burden and the glory to the cross. I take the burdens of the people who did not see their healings manifest, and I use them to put fuel on my fire. I go up the mountain and get on my face before God, and I cry out that I must have a greater revelation of the person of Jesus Christ. I must have a greater revelation of the price that Jesus paid, and I must have a greater revelation of His grace and His goodness. I must have a greater revelation of the finished work of the cross.

Recently, I was preaching in the Midwest of the U.S. and was sharing out of Acts 10:38. The church that I was preaching at has John G. Lake's personal Bible. I had the joy of reading Acts 10:38 out of this Bible. It hit me afresh when I read the word *all* that I have not arrived and that every loss is a painful reminder of this.

*How God anointed Jesus of Nazareth with the Holy Spirit and with Power, who went about doing good and healing **all** who were oppressed by the devil, for God was with him* (Acts 10:38).

When Jesus returned from the mountain after spending time with His Father, the Bible tells us that all who touched the hem of His garment were healed (see Matt. 14:36).

I need to constantly spend time with the Father, always refreshing myself and reminding myself of His goodness, love, and grace. I cannot allow any room for an offense to come into my heart.

The easy way to determine if an offense is developing in our hearts is this. If we can't learn to celebrate the miracles of others, when we need that miracle ourselves, if we end up asking, "Why them? Why not me?" then it's the start of an offense with God.

In many of the conferences I have spoken at, at the time when the miracles are happening, there may be several people standing for the same miracle. One of them will get healed, and this person will begin to celebrate, while the others in the room look with glumness in their faces, wondering why they were not healed. I can see it in their faces. *Why that person, and why not me?* Well, healing is not about us anyway; it's 100 percent by His grace. When we can shift our attention and learn to celebrate in the miracle of another, we position ourselves for that same miracle. I will often say to those that have not yet received their miracles, "I want you to give thanks and celebrate with the person who just got healed like it was your healing that you just received." When they begin to celebrate in another's breakthrough, many times their breakthroughs happen right then.

Today, after dealing with the offense that was in my heart, the greatest breakthrough that I see on a constant basis is scoliosis and any issue to do with the spine. I get so excited with every miracle, as it's my platform for my own daughter's miracle. I was in a church and three young ladies stood in front of me about my daughter's age, each with severe scoliosis. One after the other, their spines straightened, and in one case, the girl's ribs were flared. The spine moved into place along with the ribs. We must learn to celebrate, live in thanksgiving, and never be offended with God.

Encounter in Hawaii

In 2008, I was flying to Hawaii to attend a conference. I actually went to the conference just to see the speaker, as I wanted to glean from his life. I arrived at San Francisco airport and was waiting for my connection to Los Angeles. The flight was delayed, which meant I would miss my flight to Hawaii. At the last minute, I was transferred to the last remaining seat on the direct flight from San Francisco to Hawaii. I boarded, and we departed. The man next to me was a successful businessman from Hawaii. Because of the hurry in boarding the flight, I did not realize that I had been upgraded to Economy Plus until the man asked me if I normally flew Economy Plus. I answered him that I did not even realize I had been upgraded. I asked him if he normally flew Economy Plus, and he said he normally flew first class, but on purpose had downgraded himself. The people in first class don't like to talk much, but he liked to see what interesting person he might be seated next to.

He tried to debate me on politics. I said, "Sir, you have the wrong guy. I don't even know what the Senate is."

He said, "All right, let's debate religion." I knew that God had set me up.

He asked me what I do for a job. That's my favorite question to answer. To some, I say, "I'm a physician's assistant." To others, I just say, "I am a teacher or writer" (at that point, it was just e-mails I was writing). With this man, I began to share about the miracles that I get to see on a regular basis, and he was amazed. I watched *Mr. Magorium's Wonder Emporium* and then fell asleep for a while.

When I woke, he looked at me and said, "Chris, I know why you like that movie. Because you believe in the miraculous." He then asked, "You say that you see miracles all the time, but my question is this, and I want an honest answer. You shared stories of people who you have seen healed of stage 4 cancer and other diseases, but I want to know what you do when someone you are praying for dies." I asked him if he wanted the short answer or the long answer. He said, "I want the short answer, but I want it honest."

I told him that there are five things I do. The first thing that I do, with permission of the family, is pray that they are resurrected from the dead. The second thing I do, if they are not resurrected from the dead, is bury them. Then I mourn with the family. Many Christians think that mourning is wrong. We don't mourn like the world; we mourn with the knowing that we will see them again, but we can't allow our mourning to lead us to unbelief. We see, in the end of the Gospel of Mark, that if we allow our mourning to lead us to a place of unbelief, we end up focusing on what has not happened, as opposed to what has happened, and this shuts down fruitfulness. The fourth thing that I do is refuse to be offended at God, and the fifth thing that I do is get up, get back on the front line, and go look for the next impossibility to bow its knee to Jesus.

He looked at me intently and said, "I have never heard anything like this before. I was raised in Sunday school as a child, and I need to go home, find a Bible, blow off the dust, and read it again. The man had been in pain with his foot for 47 years from an accident. He had not known life for one minute without pain for this period. He had multiple pins in his ankle holding it together. I told him that I would love to pray for him, and he almost begged me. I wanted to see how eager he really was, so I made him wait. We landed and deplaned. I forgot my camera and needed to re-board, and he still waited. We went to baggage claim, got our bags, and walked outside, and he said, "OK, I am ready."

We sat on a sidewalk bench, and I just said a five-second prayer of releasing God's goodness. *God's goodness loves to manifest with the declaration of His goodness.* I said, "Move it round; test it out." I love the look on people's faces after they receive their miracle. He started slowly, and within seconds, this 60-year-old man was running around in circles on the pavement like a child, pain-free for the first time in 47 years.

As I have preached a similar message, "Today's a great day for a miracle," which is about getting over the offenses, regardless of previous results or how many times we have been prayed for, I have had many people contact me to tell me of the freedom they have personally received from this message. This is true of this message more than any other message I preach.

Many Christians have given up on ministering to the sick and dying because the burden of the loss is too hard for them to take. Instead, we must use the loss to fuel our fire, refusing to live by our experiences, because that only pulls the Gospel down to a lesser level. Rather, we must set the Gospel as our standard and live our lives to that level. The loss is the painful reminder that we have not arrived and that we need greater revelation of His goodness and grace.

Regardless of how many times I face what appears to be a defeat or how many times I get knocked down, I get myself back up and get back on the front lines. I feel like Paul sometimes—hard pressed on every side, yet not crushed; perplexed, but not in despair; persecuted, but not forsaken; struck down, but not destroyed (see 2 Cor. 4:8).

Get yourself up the mountain, get on your face before Jesus, and leave the disappointments of the past at the cross. Leave your track record with Him and start aligning yourself to the track record of Jesus Christ. I am committed to seeing an authentic Gospel displayed. I am committed to seeing the Body of Christ equipped so that believers will arise and the Church will see Jesus get all that He paid for (see Isa. 53; 1 Pet. 2:24), including seeing the sick healed, the dead raised, the lepers cleansed, and the Gospel of the kingdom preached in all nations so that cities, regions, and nations are transformed by the power of the Gospel and the Gospel of grace.

Live with the conviction that nothing is impossible with God. Live with a conviction that today is a great day for a miracle, regardless of how many times you have personally been prayed for. I declare over Charlotte regularly, "Today is a great day for a miracle, Charlotte." Live boldly enough to pray scary prayers that He can't help but show up for. I am convinced that we will see more miracles if we step out in godly confidence, knowing that all of heaven is waiting to back us up as we release the goodness of the Father. A few years ago, I prayed, "God I want to see more miracles," and He clearly answered, "Well then, pray for more people."

Many people are waiting for the hope of glory that they already possess (see Col. 1:27). We need to learn to be confident that He lives within us and His goodness is going to back us up, and we need to let

Him out, knowing that His desire to heal and His compassion that He has toward others is even greater than the desire and passion that we have for those people. We must stop waiting on Jesus to show up. When we walk in boldness and carry His confidence, trusting that He is who He said He is, we are adding our "amen" to His "yes." Let's go and release the goodness of the Father to this world and get Jesus all that He paid for.

Chapter 3

I Want More!
by Deborah Sawka Stevens

My journey into desiring and experiencing even *more* began with the simple act of opening up my heart to hear, learn, and believe that there was a deeper connection with God and the supernatural available to me. I didn't grow up in a revival-style church that often experienced an extraordinary move of God. Only on special occasions did I get a glimpse of the manifest presence of God. This typically occurred as a result of the ministry of guest speakers or when I would travel to conferences. Although these glimpses of the manifest presence of God were few in my earlier years, seeing God actively at work in people's lives in a tangible way revealed that a deeper connection with God was awaiting me. This revelation birthed a deep desire to search out the access to hidden treasures waiting for me. I was dissatisfied with the life in Christ that I was experiencing at the time because of what I'd seen and felt was possible.

I had to have more and desperately wanted to feel and experience what I had seen others experiencing. I decided that I would go to conferences that emphasized the presence of God with healings, miracles, and signs and wonders. I wasn't sure of what to expect since I had not yet been touched in the ways I had seen others experience God. I just knew that there was *something more* available from God, and whatever that looked like, I wanted it. I declared to God that I would seek and be open to receiving anything He would give me.

Ten years ago, before I moved from my home in Canada, I visited Redding, California, in 2001 to attend a conference at Bethel Church. I was in the auditorium along with over 1,000 other people receiving prayer from a guest speaker and ministry team. As the minister and the team went along praying for people, those who received prayer were dropping one by one to the floor. The floor became "littered" with people who had been slain in the Spirit. People were laughing hysterically, some crying, some wiggling, jiggling, and even bending backwards in ways that made me question if God was truly the source of their experience. (I have learned through all of the strange and unusual manifestations I encountered that some of it is just a wonder to behold. Instead of criticizing and questioning, I concluded that it is best that I just be myself, let God be God, and then just enjoy the entertainment that God provides through the manifestations that I get to witness, trusting that God will take care of the rest.)

I stood in the prayer line, waiting with great anticipation and excitement, expecting a deeper encounter with God. I closed my eyes and focused on receiving while still trying to be aware of what my physical senses were noticing. I was positioning myself as I saw others do, but I wasn't feeling anything. The minister was getting closer. I felt the person beside me hit the floor. I thought *OK, brace yourself. Here we go; it's my turn.* The minister prayed, lingered, prayed some more, and then moved on from me.

Nothing happened—or so I thought, at least. I felt nothing, and I didn't fall down like everyone else. In a crowd of 1,000 people, only a handful were still standing. I was one of the handful. Though it's painful, I would rather choose the embarrassment of being in the minority of those who don't seem to experience the manifestations rather than fake my experience.

I also wondered what was blocking me from receiving. Was there some sin in my life? I *thought* I was completely open to what God wanted to do in me. I have had many ask the same questions when they ask me to pray for them. I continued to get prayer from people who seemed to flow in the anointing for this breakthrough, but the outcome looked the same. I didn't seem to be responding any differently to His presence.

Unusual Manifestations

I wasn't giving up! My seeming lack of receiving stoked my hunger and drove me to press in. After several years on this quest, something started happening to me. No one was praying for me when it happened. It occurred when I was going about my normal day. Suddenly, I began to feel a sensation on my head. It felt like about one fourth of a cup of liquid was being poured on the top of my head. This unusual experience became a daily occurrence for me. It didn't happen at a specific time of day, but it would happen suddenly, in what would seem like a "non-spiritual" environment. I would be cleaning the house, watching a movie, working at my desk, or hiking in the mountains, for example.

At first, when I would feel it happen, I would touch the top of my head, expecting to find it wet. I'd also look up to the ceiling, thinking I would find a leak and then duck away, expecting to escape what I thought was dripping on me. Even though I experienced this manifestation for a long time, I didn't recognize that it was something spiritual and would still look in the natural for the source of liquid being poured on my head. I even wondered if I needed to see a doctor, but didn't know how to explain what I was experiencing. It was a manifestation of the Spirit at work, and I didn't have an explanation for it. It continued for the next eight years.

After years of that manifestation, a new sensation seemed to be happening to me. It felt like someone was playing with the hair on top of my head. Sometimes it tickled or made my head itch. This has happened daily ever since it began years ago, often several times a day and for about 12 years now. I've made the connection that this seems to be one of the ways I sense angels. When they come into a room, they do this to my head to let me know they are there. What I am supposed to do with that knowledge is sometimes a mystery. I have noticed that when I tell others that it is happening, they often are suddenly and deeply touched by God's presence. Sometimes I respond by touching or praying for people, and they end up having an encounter. I am sure there is much more for me to understand about when the angels make their presence known.

Spiritual Senses Activated

Although I didn't have much explanation or understanding at the time, these experiences caused me to be more in tune daily with my spiritual senses. My five physical senses were beginning to detect spiritual sensations. I physically *felt* the wind blow, when it wasn't blowing in the natural. I *felt* what seemed to be wings on my legs and arms and over the top of me. Once I even felt a giant paw on my shoulder during worship. A man came up afterward and told me a lion had been standing beside me and had put his paw on my shoulder. He didn't know about what I had experienced when he was telling me. That experience left me awestruck and relieved as I felt like my spiritual senses had been validated. Now I finally had proof that I was not just imagining these things.

In 2008, I was managing Sound Wisdom Media at Bethel. I'm so thankful for my staff, who experienced so much of this with me and allowed me the grace to press in to more when there was so much work to be done; they were Leah, Faith, Sarah, Susan, Melissa, Atasha, Maggie, Blair, Gabe, Sal, Michael, and Doug.

There were times when I would *smell* various fragrances that were not actually around me in the natural, fragrances such as sweet roses and then not so pleasant smells for me, like tobacco. I have an angel that smells like coconut, and it would often show up at work just minutes before I would arrive. Several of my staff would often smell this angel and say, when I walked through the door, "Your coconut angel arrived a few minutes ago." How can I explain these things? Some are still great mysteries to me.

The manifestations and new experiences didn't stop there. My spiritual "hearing" sense was also awakened. Sometimes I would hear an audible and comforting voice telling me something. I've heard my name called out and other sounds that are hard to describe, but in the natural were not heard by others. However, there have been a few times when I have had people turn to me and say, "Did you just hear that sound?" when there was no audible sound in the room, and I would be able to say yes! Again, in those moments, it was very encouraging that someone else had heard the sound and that I was not imagining what I was hearing.

My sense of sight in the spiritual was also affected. I began to *see* angels in different situations, some serious and some that seemed just for fun. My seeing and sensing of angels doesn't necessarily happen when I'm looking for them. More often than not, it is surprising to me to see them because it often happens as I am just going about daily life, and not when I am on a "hunt" for them.

Still More

All of these experiences were wonderful to me and even seemed natural after some time. But I still wanted *more*! I was longing for something deeper, and still the question lingered for me: *Why wasn't I overcome with God's presence like others were? Why didn't I fall down along with everyone else? Why didn't I break into laughter or have some of the other manifestations I saw people having?*

I still thought something was wrong with me since I wasn't experiencing or understanding everything that I thought I should. I still returned to those old, familiar thoughts and conclusions, which, by the way, were wrong! I wanted to be more sensitive, more able to be a carrier of His presence, but I just didn't respond to God's presence in the same way other people were responding.

"Faith" was not a new idea to me, and one of my core values quotes is *"Anything is possible, only believe"* (see Mark 9:23). I was determined that I just had to continue to position myself for receiving and that eventually Holy Spirit would come and touch me. I believed that during prayer I was still receiving something, even if it didn't look like it or I didn't "feel" it or manifest it. But still, I wanted to "feel and manifest." After years of this pursuit, certainly this was a challenge for my heart not to get discouraged. I have heard many people share with me this has been a challenge for them as well.

A New Approach

I found it hard to know what to do with people when they were manifesting, "drunk in the Spirit," while I was not feeling the same way. I decided to manage my approach while waiting in a new way and disciplined myself not to "feel" my way into good behavior, but rather "behave" my way into good feelings. Though it was awkward and uncomfortable, I pushed myself to engage, regardless of what I felt or didn't feel. For instance, when I'd find co-workers in a puddle on the floor, their bodies overcome by God's presence and acting "out of control," I'd decide to purposely make myself sit with them in order to be part of what was happening, regardless of how I felt. To be frank, sometimes all I would do is just sit there and laugh at their actions and silly ways and feel a little out of place because I didn't feel a thing.

Something New

I decided to pray for people for the very thing I wanted most. Even though it felt like I had nothing to impart, I prayed for them to be filled and deeply saturated with His presence. To my surprise, people would be overcome by God's presence and would have encounters with Him. As I prayed, they were becoming drunk in the Spirit and manifesting in all kinds of unusual ways. These people often would come back and tell me how their lives had been changed, how they had never felt that before and had never fallen down slain in the Spirit. All the things I was waiting for were being imparted to others when I prayed for them. I was being referred to as "a bartender of the wine of heaven." What? I didn't get it. How was this "flow" happening? I didn't understand how others could receive it through me while it felt like I still hadn't gotten it for myself. I needed a face-to-face with God about what was going on.

Pressing In

My desire for *more* in this area continued to increase. All kinds of signs and wonders were going on around me at Bethel Church while working and at home. At work we were expecting with great anticipation the manifestations of God's presence showing up. We began to really press into this together, and every day we were praying for *increase in this particular area*. We were spending our breaks and any extra time we had in worship and prayer.

Even while working, we would purposely press into His heart while we worked. We would play worship songs that we felt had a special anointing or lyrics that we felt opened the atmosphere for us. Doing this, we would find what we lovingly called our "portal" of connection to the Holy Spirit.

Unusual sounds, manifestations, signs, and wonders began to happen. During our worship time, we would release strange sounds, prophesy, declare, and share dreams we had. The staff would have the strangest manifestations I had seen. Regardless of how funny, silly, or weird our actions seemed, there was such freedom in what was shared. Each one was able to express, without reservation, what he or she was feeling, seeing, or sensing. The staff was becoming a closeknit family, getting healed emotionally, being delivered, forgiving people, and repenting of hidden things in their lives that they felt convicted of and that were not pleasing to God. There was such an increased level of holiness in us.

I could hardly wait to get to work in the morning because I was so excited about what God was doing in all of us. I daily went to work with an anticipation that *something* special and surprising was going to happen each day. There was an increase in the level of God's presence daily invading us. Every day different prophetic signs and wonders would happen.

My commute to work during that time was 30 minutes. I would spend that half hour drive praying in tongues and worshiping. This turned into a time of encountering God in new ways. I began to laugh while driving and feel really deeply touched by His presence in ways I had not experienced before. By the time I got to work, I would stumble through the door still laughing, and strangely, I was feeling intoxicated. My legs were weak, and I could hardly walk straight because when you laugh, all the power goes out of your legs, right? That happens to you, doesn't it? The staff would say, "Deborah! You are drunk!" I didn't feel drunk. I just thought I was laughing and the power went out of my legs. I would look at them all and say, "I'm not drunk!" (When I use the word *drunk*, I'm referring to being overtaken and intoxicated by the presence of God.) Ephesians 5:18 says, *"Do not get drunk on wine, which leads to debauchery. Instead, be filled with the Spirit"* (NIV). So being filled with the Spirit sometimes must *look* like being drunk on wine.

This laughter in me began to increase in deeper levels each day. My staff members were really being overcome by His presence in depths I had not yet seen. They would be working and suddenly some would violently fall to the floor with no warning and with a big thump, hitting tables on the way down. They miraculously would not be hurt. Some of it was really extremely funny to watch, and it seemed almost impossible that a person's body would respond to the presence of God in some of the ways the staff would.

The manifestations would make me laugh so hard that it felt like something deep was happening in me through simply laughing at the staff in the natural. I began to video and record some of the sounds and sightings, and when I would watch them again, I would experience deeper connection with the Holy Spirit. One night in the early stages of this daily happening at work, I was at home watching *The Shaggy Dog*, a Walt Disney movie with Tim Allen. I started laughing so deeply and out of *my* control at things happening in the movie; they just struck me as so funny. I couldn't stop laughing during the movie, so much so that my stomach hurt. When the laughing would subside a little, I would just think about the funny scenes in the movie. The laughter would start again and continue to the point that I was laughing so hard that it was hard to breathe. The only way I can think to explain what I was experiencing is that it felt like joy and laughter were marinating me spiritually. This was good, and I enjoyed laughing! The laughter went so deep; it felt like something opened up in me that had never been opened up before. It felt like I was a runway being prepared for the Holy Spirit to come in and land on. It was as if the angels were waving those little red wands saying, "Over here."

The experience of joy and laughter continued to increase at home and at work. It was not just in the moments when we would come together and worship, though they definitely were powerful times. There were times when we were innocently working, and the Holy Spirit would begin to work in the staff members who were labeling CDs. Several of them would just fall off their bar stools at the work counter, while trying to work. It began increasing to the point that some days we were overcome by His presence all day. We would soak and press into God's presence on our breaks and lunch hours. Conveniently, it seemed like the Holy Spirit and angels would also honor our break times. He would come like the wind through the building at 11:48 a.m. One of the staff, Atasha, while lying on the floor unable to get up, heard and blurted out, "John 11:48," not even knowing what it said. We looked up the Scripture and it read, *"If we let him go on like this, everyone will believe in him..."* (NIV). The outpouring of the Holy Spirit hit us at 11:48 a.m. every day for weeks. There was a certain ebb and flow to what we were experiencing, and when things would settle, we would all go back to work until the next time we felt His presence move into the building. We were getting all of our work done while enjoying God and playing on our lunch hour and breaks.

Joy—My Entry Point

I was beginning to make the connection that *my* entry point into feeling the presence of God more powerfully came through worship and joy. I would take pictures of the funny manifestations I witnessed, record the unusual sounds, write down the signs and wonders, and record the testimonies. At various times through the day, I would think on and look at all of these things I had valued, and they would make me laugh so deeply. Sometimes it would catapult me into deep laughter by myself in my office. The staff would come into my office to see what I was laughing about, and suddenly they would begin manifesting in their own funny ways, and some would be falling on my floor. As I recall these moments, I think the joy from recounting it all, the prayer and worship, all of it combined together, were like a marinade for me. The joy I experienced was pulling me into a deeper connection with God.

I had waited all this time to be overtaken by God and get drunk (fully intoxicated by His presence). Yet when it happened, I didn't even realize it. Though different each time, this experience became a common occurrence in my life, and I actually began to be known as a "drunk." I had a difficult time with the connotation of that word. I thought it was a derogatory statement about me because of the way we view drunks in society. When I expressed my concern about that during one of my intoxicated moments, one of my leaders told me to get over it. That was the end of those ridiculous thoughts.

While watching and hearing Pastor Bill Johnson, I learned through him to pay attention to the slightest movement of what I saw God doing. He'll stop when preaching and take time to watch when God is moving in the room. He will wait to see what God is doing and follow God's lead. God is trying to get our attention to connect with us. I realize that some of this will sound a little mystical to those who have not been exposed to it. I can just testify of what has happened to me and hope that it opens up for you the desire for your own deeper connection with the Holy Spirit, *whatever that may look like*. I hope that it plants a seed of desire that will push you to desire the *more*, the increase in joy and fullness of His presence that is available to you.

God is always doing something. It looks and feels differently to each of us. Sometimes it's funny, sometimes it's serious, but in the middle of it all is His wonderful presence. His presence manifests in different ways. He is waiting for us to find the connection—the plug-in—with the Holy Spirit. I now have my own testimony in experiencing the wine barrels from heaven. They are there for each of us to swim in and drink deeply from. They are truly a treasure and a gift, hidden for us to discover. I think most people have felt some sort of physical feeling of God's presence in their life journeys. But like me, they might not have recognized it and accounted it to God's presence. Some people might get goose bumps at some special moment, while others might experience something more identifiable, like falling down under the power of His presence. Regardless, I think there are times when we aren't aware that it is God touching us and don't attribute the experiences we have to Him because we are simply unaware of what it looks and feels like. We are all on a journey to deeper connectedness to God.

To this day, I still have not been slain in the Spirit. There are so many things I could list that I have not yet experienced. But I have hope and something to look forward to in my quest for searching for *more*! I love the wine I have discovered and value the pleasures of drinking His presence. I also am looking to discover the other treasures and experiences I have heard of or sense are possible. This topic is just one of the many facets of our relationship with our Father that I wanted to share because this one seems to tangibly minister to us, and I have had so many people come and share their pursuit of wanting to drink the wine of heaven. I know God wants *more* for me, even *more* than I do, and I am continuing on my search for what He has hidden and is waiting for me to discover. Psalm 16:11 reads, *"You have made known to me the path of life; you will fill me with joy in your presence, with eternal pleasures at your right hand"* (NIV).

Enjoy His presence!

Part 2

LOVING OTHERS

"There the Lord commanded the blessing...."
—Psalm 133:3b

Maybe one of the reasons the Lord told us to consider the ant (see Prov. 6:6) is that they accomplish such great things through their cooperativeness and unity. What could an isolated ant ever do? Whether between spouses, siblings, congregants, or friends, our human relationships make up the stuff of life. Relationships have the power either to heighten our connection with God or to hinder it. Great reward awaits those who cultivate true connectedness and covenantal relationship with others.

Chapter 4

COMFY
IN THE CLUSTER
by Pam Spinosi

When I was considering moving from overseas to Redding, California, of course I consulted my best friend, Jane. We have the kind of friendship that attracts the attention of heaven. Once, when I returned home from my first year abroad, just weeks after her wedding, as we sat together catching up in her living room, the presence of the Lord seemed to come right into our midst. "Jane," I said, "Do you feel that?"

"Yes, dear," she said, "You brought it."

"No, I didn't!" I protested, "I didn't feel it until now with you."

There is something about the sweetness of true covenant friendship that invites the Lord to join in. Every time I need to make a major life-changing decision, I can count on Jane to confirm it or have a word or impression from the Lord that really helps me. And often in her hectic mommy world, when she most needs to remember that God loves her, I seem to phone her, and she takes it as a nudge from God that He truly does have her back. Though our circumstances are very different, we share a true spirit-to-spirit bond, and we know that our mutually satisfying friendship is a gift from the Lord to us both.

So Jane had a word for me as we pondered my next *leap across the pond*: "I keep hearing, 'The wine is in the cluster.'" And I knew she was right. Though I'd always been in fellowship and always had a home church, I had been feeling a bit alone, a bit out there by myself. Much of what I'd done in life erred on the side of individual more than corporate, and I was ready for a deeper level of teamwork. So I took the plunge and came to Bethel, ready to immerse myself in something that was greater than me, ready to be part of a bigger picture.

Created for the Cluster

While there are many reasons we need to be a functioning part of a church family, on a personal level, we all just plain need others. We were designed that way. We were created for the cluster. But being in the cluster can sometimes be uncomfortable. We can get a foot in the eye. Maybe that's why so much of the Bible is devoted to human relationships and how to navigate them. The importance of our relationship with others cannot be overestimated. We are told that if we honor our parents, we will live long (see Eph. 6:2-3); if we honor our spouses, our prayers will be answered (see 1 Pet. 3:7); if we forgive, we'll be forgiven (see Luke 6:37); and if we give, we'll receive (see Luke 6:38). Our relationship with the Lord can be hindered by our treatment of or reaction to others to the extent that we can't even give Him our gift—our worship—until we go make it right with the ones we've offended (see Matt. 5:24).

The benefits of our relationships with others are many. One can chase merely 1,000; two can chase 10,000 (see Matt. 18:19). The writer of Ecclesiastes asserted that, *"two are better than one…"* (Eccles. 4:9). God, Himself, even when He was in full, unbroken fellowship with the man, Adam, in the garden, said that it was *"not good for the man to be alone…"* (Gen. 2:18 NIV) and centuries later promised through the psalmist to *"set the solitary in families"* (Ps. 68:6). God had to confound the languages of the people building the tower of Babel. They were so unified that nothing could stop them from their evil intentions (see Gen. 11). God's blessing is found where there is unity (see Ps. 133:3), and He even promises to be wherever two or more are gathered in His name (see Matt. 18:20). His great heart is for family, and churches are meant to resemble His model of family: people experiencing covenantal relationships with one another in love, service, loyalty, and genuine godly affection. Marriage is not the only relationship involving covenant. We are to cultivate covenantal relationships with friends as well.

Comparison

With all the reasons we have to come together in fellowship, develop friendships, and maintain close ties to our families, what stops us? Why did Cain kill his own brother? (See Genesis 4.) What irked the older brother in the parable of the Prodigal Son? (See Luke 15.) How come the laborers griped when the newbies got the same amount—a penny—as they did after laboring in the sun all day? (See Matthew 20:1-16.) What prompted Peter to ask, *"What about this man?"* (John 21:21). I say it was comparison. We look at our brother and ask, "Why him? Why not me?" Jesus never seemed to condone this type of thinking. In His parables, He has the loving father gently reassure the older brother that he, too, mattered, but that it was important to celebrate the return of his sibling (see Luke 15:31). And Jesus has the master ask the laborers, *"Are you resentful because I'm generous?"* (Matt. 20:15 CEV). His answer to Peter was essentially, "What's it to you? You follow Me" (see John 21:22).

Comparing ourselves with others can lead to discontentment. While we may aspire to more and "to covet the best gifts," we don't have the right to despise who God has made us to be. He makes that clear in Isaiah 45:9:

> *Woe to him who strives with his Maker! Let the potsherd strive with the potsherds of the earth! Shall the clay say to him who forms it, "What are you making?" Or shall your handiwork say, "He has no hands?"*

We have to be the best "us" we can. No one else can be me. That we all have unique sets of fingerprints should tell us that we are different by design. God doesn't make clones. I have a few coasters made of Belgian lace, fashioned meticulously by the knobby fingers of Belgian artisans, hunched over a pillow on which they carefully place and replace pins to twist the threads that form the beautiful patterns. You can tell their creations are crafted by hand: they are not uniform. I treasure them. The perfectly formed designs in synthetic thread made by machines don't even compare. I'm happy that we haven't found a way to make people by machine. We are all crafted by the Master Artisan. Though we are not entirely "uniform," we are unique and beautiful. If we can revel in the kind of "pot" the Maker has formed us to be, if we can receive from Him our individual identity, we can more easily rejoice in the uniqueness of those around us. If I know I am a flowerpot, and my role is to house the beautiful flowers, I don't need to wish I was the golf bag that carries the clubs. That's not my role, and I can let the golf bag do that job and be happy that I bring joy to my "owner" by being who I am.

Competition

Another thing that harms our relationships is competition. We see that a lot in the Old Testament. We see Leah, the unloved spouse, conspiring to win her husband's attentions through offering her son's mandrakes (see Gen. 30:16). We see in First Samuel 1:6, Peninnah taunting the loved, but childless Hannah, and in Genesis we see Jacob and his mother devising a scheme to get his father to give him his brother's blessing after he got his birthright (see Gen. 27:5-17). I think the problem in all those situations was a fear of lack. There could only be *one* favorite wife; there was only *one* firstborn birthright. They had to be competitive to get what they wanted. In our case, when we find that competitive spirit at work, it's because deep down we think there is not enough. "If he gets the cookie, there won't be one left for me." That, of course, is not the truth. Jesus said, *"In my Father's house are many mansions..."* (John 14:2). In Revelation 5:10, we find out that we have *all* been made *"to be a kingdom and priests to our God"* who *"will reign upon the earth"* (NASB). There is room for each of us to be the favorite, each to get the birthright.

Mistrust

Anyone who has tried to rescue a feral cat knows how hard it is to get the cat to come inside and get warm, come near and get a reassuring cuddle, get close enough to eat the nourishing meal. Though it needs all those things, its fear and mistrust keep it from them. The same happens to people who have enclosed themselves in walls of fear or mistrust. They interpret everything through their skewed lenses. Hurt people build walls. Whole people are able to allow others in. If we have to forgive 70 times 7, it's not so we can be pushovers. It's so that we will not inflict our own souls with the sickness of unforgiveness, offense, or cold love. To have true relationship, we have to be vulnerable with one another, and we cannot do that if we harbor mistrust. What we are ultimately saying when we build walls to keep others out is that we cannot be sure our heavenly Father will protect us. Will He really take care of us, or do we have to fear others?

Be Really, Really Loved

The solution to all these hindrances to relationship is love, not that we need to love more, but that we need to know more that we are loved by God. The revelation that He abundantly loves us makes all the difference. My perfect picture of one who knows he is loved is Simon, the youngest son of a couple I knew from South Africa. As his mom prepared dinner and I talked with his dad over a cup of coffee, Simon slipped under his dad's arm, grinned, dunked his cookie in his dad's mug, took a bite, slid off Dad's lap and ran off to resume his play. His dad didn't skip a beat. He didn't mind at all—and Simon knew it. He was a much-loved son. His dad's coffee was his to enjoy. I picture that incident when I want to remember that I am a much-loved daughter. I can dunk my cookie in the Father's coffee. I can approach Him even if I don't seem to have been as fruitful as my brother or sister. Like them both, I have the same access: it's all by grace. It's all by what Jesus did for us. When I know I am loved, I don't have to compare myself with others. I know that just who I am is what God wants me to be. He made me.

When I know I am loved, I don't have to compete. There is enough for me, too. Simon's brother and sister are equally loved, so they aren't bothered by their dad's affection for him. They have it, too.

And when I know I'm loved, I can rise up to be all He made me to be. Jonathan was a great man. He did not have to envy David. He recognized the anointing and call on him and accepted it. Jonathan loved him in covenant friendship because he was a man of faith and he knew David by the spirit. But he was not an underling. He was a great man, himself. So was John the Baptist. Jesus called him the greatest of the prophets. But John recognized that he was not the Christ and that Jesus was. He had no problem "decreasing so He would increase" (see John 3:30). That did not mean he was not great. In fact, he was. He knew who he was, but he knew who was greater.

Jesus said to love the Lord our God with all our hearts, souls, minds, and strength and to love our neighbors as ourselves (see Luke 10:27). I think we have to start with receiving God's love for us. We love Him because He first loved us. When we are overcome by His love for us, it's easy to love others. It's then that we can avoid offense (love suffers long, is not easily provoked). It's then that we can esteem others more highly than ourselves (love vaunts not itself). When we *know* that we are loved, we can look at the things of others, not of ourselves (see Phil. 2:4). Had Joseph's brothers felt every bit as loved as he, they may not have resented him. (See Genesis 37:11.)

I once heard Graham Cooke say that our job is to be really, really loved. That rang true to me. Then we can love back without hypocrisy or measure. Being loved by God is the salve of our hearts. Jesus loved us with a great love and washed us with His blood (see Rev. 1:5), and we truly are complete in Him, able to love others with the love that we receive.

Identity in the Father's Love

Young ladies get their identity from their fathers. I have known gorgeous women who are insecure about their looks; some of them end up destroying their health through disorders like anorexia or bulimia. I have also known young women who I would label as slightly attractive, at best, but who exude a perfect confidence and profound assurance of their own beauty and worth. I used to wonder how they could see themselves that way. Then I discovered the clue: they each had a wonderful daddy who had lavished such praise on them their entire lives that they were convinced of their beauty and preciousness. We can all have that. Though we may not have benefited from the love of adoring fathers throughout our childhoods, we can get the assurance of our worth from our heavenly Father. And how much more so? To recognize, experience, and fathom His unending love for us should be a lifelong quest. It is becoming one for me; I have recognized the need. For healing and transformative power, nothing equals a revelation of His love for us.

If my identity is in God and my acceptance is from Him, I can give others what I've received from Him: pure love. I can give them a new slate every day. Instead of thinking, "Oh, he's always late," I can "believe all things," as instructed in First Corinthians 13:7, and allow him to change and be on time. I don't have to have negative expectations of him based on the past. I can cheer her on when it's her turn to "get the cookie." I don't have to vie with her for the seat at the table. There is a seat for me, too.

This is a great prayer to pray until we are saturated with the answer:

...that you...may be able to comprehend with all the saints what is the width and length and depth and height—to know the love of Christ which passes knowledge; that you may be filled with all the fullness of God (Ephesians 3:17-19).

Chapter 5

True Intimacy
by Sheri Downs

"Sheri, it's over! I have my things packed, and I am leaving."

I did not realize that the spoken word carried such potential for devastation until that day. Those 12 little words changed the course of my life forever.

After a 15-and-a-half-year marriage, two kids, a dog, two cars, and a mortgage, my "first love," the love of my life, decided he did not love me anymore. Now for someone who was all about "true intimacy" and love, this came as quite a blow, and it completely turned my safe little life upside down.

I have always fancied myself a person who knows how to love and how to make others feel special. But when my lover, my best friend, and the person on this planet who knew me better than anyone else told me, "It's over," it made me question what intimacy and love are really all about.

It has been almost 16 years since that unforgettable day in the parking lot of Bethel Church, and my journey to find the true meaning of intimacy continues to be an ongoing quest. Along the way, I have learned some valuable truths and practical ways to cultivate a lifestyle of intimacy with God and those around me.

Recognize the Lie

The first truth I discovered completely obliterated a lie I had believed during my entire relationship with David—that intimacy is all about sex. Coming from an extremely dysfunctional childhood, I thought sex was the ultimate form of intimacy and that whenever I married, I would keep my husband happy as long as I performed well in the bedroom. Hormonal teens tend to think differently than the rest of society, and this is exactly what we were. I was thinking about sex, and so was he. What we did not realize in our two years of dating was that we had fallen in love as a result of spending hours upon hours talking about our hopes and dreams for our lives together. We were building a strong sense of intimacy during that time, letting each other know what was going on in our hearts and not hiding anything. He was the first person I had been totally vulnerable with, sharing the depths of dysfunction that was my childhood. He reciprocated by opening up his inner world, and we developed a bond that connected our hearts long before we ever connected our bodies in marriage. So when we married at the ages of 20 and 19, the foundation of our marriage was true intimacy and not sex. However, being an inexperienced hormonal adolescent, I did not know how to cultivate intimacy on a *consistent* basis. I still believed that intimacy meant sex.

Now that I am older and a littler wiser and have had tremendous teaching and insight, I realize that the foundations of true intimacy have little to do with sex. Don't get me wrong. I do believe that sex is certainly a part of intimacy, but it is only a small portion and then only between a husband and wife. I believe God desires for us to have intimacy with Him and others as well, and that has absolutely nothing to do with sex. I've heard it said that intimacy means "into-me-you-see." I love this definition because it paints a clear picture of what is happening when two people are intimate. It would have been nice to have this teaching when I was young and developing my relationship with my husband.

David and I always had fun together because we pursued a lot of the same passions, sharing our dreams, wants, and desires. We opened up our hearts and saw deep inside one another. We had nothing hidden in those days, and we openly communicated how our words and actions affected one another. In short, we were "falling in love." I now believe, however, that individuals do not fall in love; they "grow" in love, and that really is what intimacy is all about. I realize now that we were on to something. If I could go back and capture those times, I would, knowing now that we were discovering, quite by accident, what true intimacy consists of.

As the years quickly passed and the pressures of married life began to settle in around us, we found ourselves too busy and too tired to continue spending hours upon hours sharing our hearts and dreams. We only had the time and energy to raise our young family and deal with the day in and day out problems and situations that define many marriages.

Somewhere along the journey, we took a bite out of a piece of fruit from the wrong tree: we believed the lie that, in order to appear happily married, we had to hide what was really going on deep down inside of our hearts. So we hid behind the routine of daily life and busied ourselves dealing with finances, raising our children, and going through the motions of marriage to the extent that we lost the communication of what we were really feeling in the innermost depths of our souls. Our sex life was flourishing, yet we ceased to share our dreams and desires with one another; in fact, we lost the ability to dream together. Our intimate connection was gone long before the devastation of that fateful day.

When things started falling apart, my husband and I sought counseling, inner healing, and all the other tools available to us since neither of us believed in divorce. However, we had lost that intimate connection regarding what was really going on toward one another at the depths of who we truly are. We focused on the fruit, but failed to expose the root that was actually dying—intimacy. We had clothed ourselves with our responsibilities and no longer granted one another access to the nakedness of our vulnerability and true feelings.

Even as I write this and reflect upon what went horribly wrong in what should have been my most intimate relationship, I am realizing that the majority of people go through life so desperately wanting true love, but never really knowing how to go about cultivating intimacy: It takes time, effort, commitment, patience, vulnerability, and intention. In our 21st-century world, where we live in a microcosm of convenience, fast food, and microwave meals, that sounds like way too much work.

Let God Redeem

So once divorce became a harsh reality, I began to grapple with the daunting question: "Am I ever going to know true intimacy?" I do not believe God condones divorce, but I do believe He will use whatever we yield to Him. The first thing I had to yield was the security of the artificial world I had created for myself by learning what it looks like to get to know the real me. Let me explain. I lived in a world of denial for most of my life; it was the only way I knew how to survive. From the age of 4 until I was 12 years old, I was sexually molested by a family member who threatened me that I must never tell anyone. The only way I knew how to remain safe was to build a fantasy world and never let anyone in close enough to know the real truth. In essence, I lived a double life.

At church and school, I would be the good little Christian girl, hiding my pain behind my athletic abilities, my talent for singing, and my fake smile. In other words, I learned how to perform for love and acceptance. No one knew what was going on at home, not even my parents. Thus, I became quite the performer. In fact, I performed so well that I even fooled myself into believing that my life was normal and I just had to go on living with my dirty little secret. After all, if anyone else knew, I would not be accepted and would end up alone. It was not until years later, when all of these hidden secrets came rushing to the surface for the first time in my life, that I had to be real and honest with myself and admit I was pretty messed up. This revelation led me to pursue intimacy with God.

Obviously, God knows everything about me, but because I was so good at denial and performance, I thought I was actually hiding my secrets from God, Himself. Little did I know that God was actually drawing me out into the open to expose the lies I had built my life around so He could clothe me with the truth of His love. I offered up to Him all that was left within me, which was not much: shattered dreams, a broken heart, and a very dim future. I no longer had to perform for acceptance because I discovered my true identity as a daughter of God. In exchange for all my brokenness, He gave me hope, joy, faith, and love.

This time around, I decided that the only foundation I would build my life upon was God. I put my complete trust in Him and Him alone. The psalmist made this clear when he said in Psalm 127:1, *"Unless the Lord builds the house, its builders labor in vain. Unless the Lord watches over the city, the watchmen stand guard in vain"* (NIV). I knew that I was very capable of building many things, but I no longer wanted my life to be the product of my own abilities, performance, or selfish efforts. I had tried that once. I wanted to build in such a way that the *"glory of this latter house shall be greater than of the former,"* like the Lord declares, and that in my house God will similarly *"grant peace"* (Hag. 2:9). This would prove to be a multi-step process.

The first step I took on my journey of finding intimacy with God and myself was to take advantage of a tool we offer at Bethel Church called a Sozo. Sozo is an inner healing ministry that goes into deep places of the heart that are bound up in lies. The Holy Spirit then reveals the truth and unlocks the prison doors, releasing the captive heart and pouring love and hope into places that were dead and hopeless.

Many lies that I had believed were uncovered during my Sozo, and I began a process of facing the pain I had endured as a child that I had long ago learned how to cover up and deny. The first thing I had to do was take an honest look within and release myself from the guilt and shame that had become my best friends. Once I did that, I was able to see myself as God created me. Instead of carrying around a deep, dark, dirty little secret, I was free to be me, no longer needing to perform in order to be accepted. I was able to embrace the truth that I am an innocent, pure, beautiful, fun, joyful pleasure to be around.

Learning to Trust

The next step was to begin to trust people again, and that was not going to be easy. I certainly believe in boundaries, but I took boundaries to a whole new level by constructing walls that would keep me safe from anyone ever hurting me again. The problem was that the walls I built to keep myself safe simply isolated me by keeping people out. I discovered that I was still dying a slow death, even though I had received so much love and freedom from being intimate with God and myself. The Lord showed me that in order for me to continue to walk out my freedom, I must begin to let people in and experience intimacy with other human beings.

This meant taking risks and opening up to others who could possibly hurt me and cause me more pain. I also had to realize that the strategy of the enemy was to keep me bound up in the isolation by making me think that I could only go through life on a surface level with the very people God had chosen for me to be in relationship with. The solution hinged on the revelation that I needed to surround myself with people who would love me for me because what I was actually longing for was true intimacy with others.

We were created for community and cannot be fully functioning apart from it. When speaking to the Colossians, Paul admonishes them by saying:

> *Therefore as God's chosen people, holy and dearly loved, clothe yourselves with compassion, kindness, humility, gentleness, and patience. Bear with each other and forgive whatever grievances you may have against one another. Forgive as the Lord forgave you. And over all these virtues, put on love which binds them all together in perfect unity. Let the peace of Christ rule in your hearts, since as members of one body you were called to peace. And be thankful* (Colossians 3:12-15 NIV).

I would have to choose intimacy in community, not expect that it would just happen to me.

Deciding that true intimacy with others was worth the risk, I took a step of faith and immersed myself in church culture and Bethel School of Supernatural Ministry. I became a student and began building relationships with those who had the same passion for the presence of the Lord, a passion that still has my affections. Even though it was challenging for me at first, I built some lifelong friendships by opening myself up to intimacy with others and allowing them to see inside of me. Much to my surprise, they love the real me. It is extremely refreshing and rewarding to know I can be real with those the Lord has put in my life and know that they will confront me in love when necessary, ask me tough questions when it is uncomfortable, and not let me get away with hiding behind anything.

I have discovered the true meaning of intimacy with God, myself, and those God has placed in my life; I am no longer afraid of being vulnerable or real, and I am cultivating this daily by making it a lifestyle, one propagated by daily communing with Papa God. This takes on various forms, but tangibly consists of personal time with Him through worship, quiet time, and reading the Word, being intentional about building true relationships with those around me, creating a safe place for others to be real, and genuinely loving people the way Papa God, the Holy Spirit, and Jesus love me.

For a person who had major trust issues and a broken and warped sense of intimacy, I have had tremendous breakthrough. I am quite confident that if my paradigm can make such a drastic shift, then anyone who is willing to open up and be real with God, themselves, and others will also experience a whole new world of love and true intimacy.

Chapter 6

LETTERS FROM A SHOEBOX
by Stefanie Overstreet

November 9, 1997 Entry

Dear Future Husband,

Hi, I keep wondering who you are, where you are in the present, what you look like, and if I know you now. I look forward to meeting you so much. . . .

My journey in preparing for marriage began with these lines in my 12-year-old scrawl on a sheet of notebook paper. This was the first letter I wrote to my future husband. After a childhood of loving fairy tales and dressing up as a princess, I was already dreaming of who I would marry in my God-given beautiful love story. I decided to start writing letters to channel my curiosity and record thoughts I wanted to someday share with him. My romantic pre-teen heart also loved the idea of surprising my husband on our wedding day with a stack of letters I had been writing and saving for years in a shoebox under my bed.

At the time when I wrote the first letter, I was attending a girls' discipleship group that taught me how to value myself and what healthy relationships look like. That group also helped me set a foundation for qualities I would look for in a spouse. Maybe it was because I was mature for my age, but I developed a desire to navigate the years before I met my spouse with few regrets. It was important to me to save myself, not just in body, but also my heart and emotions, for that special man I would meet someday. My heart's desire was to honor God and my future spouse. I wanted to be able to look back on those preparation years and know that I had made choices that contributed to a healthy marriage.

Most of my high school years were spent growing in relationship with God, learning more about myself, and developing core values for dating relationships. I didn't date much in high school, not really because of a conscious choice, but mainly because I wasn't pursued. Being pursued was a core value of mine, so it was painful feeling like I wasn't "noticed" during those years. Looking back now, I can see I wasn't really "wired" for the kind of teenage dating that happens before you're in a stage of life where you're ready to get married. I learned what it looked like for me to delight myself in God—in His faithfulness—and trust Him with the desires of my heart (see Ps. 37:4). I wrote my future husband a lot of letters in those years. It was cathartic to share my thoughts, feelings, and experiences in a raw, honest way with someone who would someday love and accept me. Writing letters really gave purpose to that season in my life, especially when I felt lonely.

Somewhere in the transition from my later years in high school to attending university, I began to see a few themes emerge in my journey. The first theme was that every step and experience was preparation. I really began to value the process when I realized that each day, each new revelation, each letter I wrote were all preparation that brought me one step closer to meeting my future spouse. A mentor once told me, "God never wastes an experience." This statement really encouraged me each step of the way, when I was hopeful and dreaming about the future and also when I experienced disappointment as I did begin to date. No matter the experience, I trusted that God would use it to tutor me and move me forward in my journey toward marriage.

A second theme was hope. A key Scripture that influenced my journey is Hebrews 10:23, *"Let us hold fast the confession of our hope without wavering, for He who promised is faithful"* (ESV). When you have hope, it influences how you live. In order for hope to influence how you live, you need to know specifically what you're hoping for and what God is saying about it.

While I was attending university, I got specific about what I was hoping for. I narrowed down what I was looking for in a spouse to three non-negotiable characteristics: a living, Spirit-filled relationship with Jesus; a call to the nations, specifically Africa; and a heart that passionately worships Jesus. I had also realized some important core values that would help me to identify the kind of man I would want to marry. I mentioned in one of my letters that I thought I would know he is the right man for me because of his value to protect my heart and guard my purity and how he would lead me by seeking to follow Christ in our relationship. Being specific about these aspects helped give my hope focus and direction. These aspects were the confession of my hope.

More important was my confession of hope in God and His faithfulness. I hadn't come across Hebrews 10:23 when I first began writing the letters, but I can see now that hope in His faithfulness was the foundation of my journey from the beginning. I wrote letters to my future husband because my hope rested on *"He who promised is faithful."* I started my journey by hoping in the nature of God's loving faithfulness. As my journey progressed, I began to gather His promises to me regarding this part of my life. I discovered His promises in many ways, but the most pivotal promise came to me in the first prophetic word I'd ever received.

During the spring of my freshman year in college, I had just received word that I was accepted into my university's competitive nursing program. I felt called to become a registered nurse and work with children and eventually care for orphans in Africa. In the short time since I had started to date, it had become clear that finding a man with a call and passion for Africa equal to mine might prove to be a challenge. I found myself learning to really trust and hope in God's faithfulness for my life—that I could both be married and still be faithful to my call to Africa.

I had just started attending an on-campus Christian group, and a guest speaker from Youth With A Mission shared one night. During ministry time, I received my first-ever prophetic word from her. The gist of the word was this: She saw a picture of me in a nurse's uniform doing medical mission work and felt that the nations would be open to me if I asked. Also, she said the Lord had a running mate and ministry partner for me. She encouraged me not to let just anyone sweep me off my feet because the right one would make my heart sing. Wow! The Lord spoke through that word so specifically about two of the greatest desires in my heart. Since the prophetic was new to me, I was profoundly moved by how much the Lord knew my heart and how gracious He was to encourage my desires. That word became His promise to me.

My hope in God's faithfulness to His promise really did change the way I lived. That prophetic word showed me that He cared enough to speak to the desires of my heart, and I was learning to trust Him more. Trusting Him meant I could live with a greater sense of peace and security. I didn't have to worry about who I would meet, when it would take place, or how it would work out. I also experienced a newfound hope. This hope allowed me to co-labor with God in His purposes for my life. Carrying His promises made me an active participant in my journey toward marriage. I didn't feel like I was at a standstill waiting for God to bring the right man into my life. I was able to go forward in my life with confidence that I was on the right track. Because I knew He was faithful, I pursued with full abandon greater relationship with Him and a nursing degree focused on caring for children. I learned to trust that as I pursued my dreams of caring for orphans in Africa, God was working all the details together and my path would cross with my future spouse in God's perfect timing.

While in my senior year of college, I faced a time of testing. Proverbs 13:12 says, *"Hope deferred makes the heart sick, but a desire fulfilled is a tree of life"* (ESV). At this time in my life, my hope was deferred. I was faced with starting to explore decisions about where I would live and work after graduation.

February 1, 2007 Entry

Pretty soon I'll be figuring out what to do next—after graduation that is. It's kinda weird making plans for the future since I'd always imagined I would've met you by now. . . . It's been really tough without you lately. I really desire your companionship right now.

For almost ten years, I had been trusting God, praying, and writing letters to my future husband. I still had never been in even a remotely serious relationship. When I first started writing the letters, I'd promised to save my first kiss for him on our wedding day. Now I found myself doubting that I'd ever meet someone who would value and want to honor my promise. Even though I knew I was young and had plenty of time to meet someone, I was feeling lonely, scared, and discouraged about the future. Making life-altering decisions about my future had me wishing for my lifelong companion. The future was exciting in some ways, but I was just plain tired of being alone and afraid to make decisions about my future alone. I started questioning myself and my standards, wondering if I was expecting too much. Fear and loneliness had me considering dating men that I knew in my heart didn't represent the man I'd dreamed of and prayed about—the one who would fulfill the promises God had spoken so clearly to me and who I was supposed to be trusting God for. At my lowest point, I was less than a year away from meeting my husband, Chris. For me, the test really did come just before the fulfillment of the promise.

Though it was a challenging time in my life, and sometimes I wish I could change it, I'm convinced it was a key part of the final preparation before I met my husband. Through the grace and mercy of

God, and with the help of close friends, I realized that the time when my hope was deferred wasn't time to give up. It was time to fight for my hope in the faithfulness of God to His promises. Practically, this meant meditating on Scriptures like Hebrews 10:23 and prophetic words like the one mentioned earlier. I also reminded myself that God's love for me meant I wasn't alone and didn't need to be afraid. A renewed experience of His love for me banished loneliness and fear. This time of testing gave merit to my hope and increased my determination not to settle for less than what I believed Him for.

A key element involved in the final months leading up to meeting Chris was risk-taking. In fact, taking a risk was how I actually met Chris. I don't mean to sound like risk-taking is a formula or criteria for meeting a spouse. I do see it as an area that the Lord knew I needed to grow in to really be ready to meet my husband. I had always run the other way when faced with taking risks. (How ironic that I ended up marrying a man who is practically a professional risk-taker!) At the end of my senior year in college, I decided to take a huge risk to pursue my dreams of nursing and ministering to orphans in Africa. I decided to apply for a nursing job in Redding in hopes of one day attending Bethel School of Supernatural Ministry and eventually doing medical mission work in Africa. At the time, it meant moving out of state by myself and potentially starting out working in an area of nursing I wasn't passionate about.

A close friend who also had decided to move to Redding came with me when I interviewed for nursing positions two months before graduation. On that trip, I started to see the fulfillment of His promises. Through the favor of God, I was offered a nursing position in pediatrics that I initially wasn't eligible for as a new graduate. I remember sitting in the prayer house at Bethel just amazed at how God was bringing my dreams to pass. Here I was planning to move to Redding and attend Bethel Church while working as a pediatric nurse—my dream job—and having a close friend as a roommate. I spent time thanking God and rejoicing in His faithfulness. And, with my hope in full force, I reminded Him there was still one more promise yet to be fulfilled.

By the time I'd moved to Redding a few months later, the Lord had been speaking to me about evangelism—an area in my walk with Him where I hadn't seen much fruit. He'd recently spoken some promises to me about bearing fruit in this area, but I knew in order for it to come to pass, I was going to have to take some more risk. As soon as I moved to Redding, I became involved in the outreach ministry. It was serious risk-taking for me to get involved in a ministry where I had such little comfort and confidence. I'd heard about a Back-to-School Backpack Giveaway that Bethel Church was hosting. I figured this event would be a great way to get to know some of the families and children who might be my patients at the local hospital.

I met Chris at the first meeting for the Backpack Giveaway about a month after I moved to Redding. Some of his key leaders in outreach befriended me, and I was invited to help them administrate the Backpack Giveaway during the month before the event. As I spent time with them, they shared about Chris' heart to raise money for orphaned children in Africa: Heroes of the Nation in Kenya, specifically. As I got to know him, I witnessed his passion and worship for God, his love for people, and his dedication to reaching all of Africa, including children. It wasn't long before I had developed interest in Chris, and I was telling the Lord, "Now this is the kind of man I've been hoping for!" There was no question he fit the qualities I felt were important to me.

After the Backpack Giveaway, I joyfully discovered that my interest in Chris was mutual, and he began to pursue me. A love story began that surpassed every hope and desire in my heart. I experienced the "tree of life" Proverbs talks about, a monument in my life to the faithfulness of God. I saw how He addressed every necessary detail in bringing us together. Like the layers of a painting, I could see how God had used the letters I'd written, the Scriptures and prophetic words I held onto, challenges I overcame, and experiences I walked through to create a masterpiece that reflected the beauty of the Artist.

It would take an entire book to convey all the details of the story, but I do want to share what stands out in my memory. When our relationship became serious, Chris gave me a promise ring—not a promise of a future engagement—but to promise the core values he had for our relationship. He promised me three things to the best of his ability: to guard my heart, to protect my purity, and to seek God for the leading and guiding in the timing of our relationship. I can't describe how much this meant to me other than to say that it was confirmation for me that he was the man I wanted to marry. I was amazed how God knew those specifics were important to me, so much so that Chris' words were almost identical to what I'd written in one of my letters, a letter he had never read. Chris also shared with me that because of his value for sexual purity, he'd chosen not to kiss a woman again on the lips until his wedding day. I was so glad to be dating a man who had the same core value I did—and I had to laugh that God certainly hadn't overlooked that detail despite my previous doubts!

I realize everyone has varying opinions on God's involvement in relationships and whether there is "one right person" out there or whether there are multiple potential spouses we could find happiness with. Chris and I were confident of the hand of God in our lives and the coming together of our relationship, but we also experienced the beautiful freedom of choosing each other as well. I don't mean for the sharing of my journey to draw that delineation. What's more important is that God is bigger than our opinions and expectations. I think my journey shows that it's His good pleasure to give us the desires of our hearts and that He is great enough to take care of the details that really matter to us. In fact, in my experience, He is great enough to lead us into a relationship that is far better than we could dream of or imagine. It's not that my relationship with Chris and his qualities are exactly what I'd imagined in every way. But who Chris is as a person and the beauty of our relationship are better and different than I could have imagined.

While we were engaged and preparing to be married, I thoroughly enjoyed writing Chris letters, knowing that he would get to read them in a few short months.

March 31, 2008 Entry

I'm really looking forward to giving you these letters. I hope they are able to give you an idea of how much I've loved you, prayed for you and dreamed about you in the last ten years. I can't wait to see the look on your face when I present these letters to you!

During this time, the letters provided a place for reflection on the preparation and journey toward marriage. In retrospect, the experience of writing the letters, saving them, and preparing to give them to my husband paralleled my journey in preparing for marriage—each lesson learned and experience walked through collectively was about to culminate at the end of this particular journey of preparation.

Chris and I were married June 21, 2008, and yes, we did share an enthusiastic first kiss in front of friends and family. I kept the letters I had been writing a secret from Chris. That was very tough at times! And after ten and a half years of writing, I surprised him on our wedding day with a stack of 74 letters. Seeing the joyful surprise on his face and the tears in his eyes was an incredibly meaningful reward that I will never forget.

Part 3

LIVING LIFE

Where to go from here. . .?

The steps of a good man are ordered by the Lord,
and He delights in his way. —Psalm 37:23

The large questions of life like "Why am I here?" and "What should I do?" take on new meaning and importance for the Christian set on living a fruitful life with God. But sometimes we just have to take ourselves a little less seriously—and take our confidence in God a lot more seriously. Like the girl in this photo, we can find some fun and whimsy along the way, even as we advance in increasing responsibility in our roles as co-laborers with the King of the universe, our loving God. We get to walk in the path already prepared for us from the foundation of the world, yet we also get to choose. What a glorious paradox. Could it be He has a divine destination for us and we get to choose how—and whether and to what extent—we get there?

Chapter 7

CALLED, GUIDED, AND PREPARED
by Paul Manwaring

I will never forget receiving my call to "full-time ministry." Oh, how the definition of that phrase has changed in my heart since that first moment. I was attending an Evangelism Explosion Trainer's Conference in Southampton, England, in September 1976. At the closing service, the preacher, Reverend Vic Jacobson, preached on the life of Dr. David Livingstone. The charge he left us with that night was this:

> *Send me anywhere Lord,*
> *Only go with me.*
> *Lay any burden upon me,*
> *Only sustain me.*

Sever any tie that binds,
Save that which binds my heart
to thyself and thy service.

I wrote those verses in the front of my Bible, and they became my prayer and my call. Vic Jacobson had left an indelible mark on my soul; ironically this man, saved in Winchester prison, would be my guidance as I walked through a career in prison work, supposedly on my way to my call.

Upon my return from that weekend, I wrote to a man who was to become my grandfather-in-law, the Reverend Stuart Harris. He was a career missionary, having been president of the European Christian Mission. Another strange coincidence was that it was he who brought Richard Wormbrandt home from Romania to London—Richard, who would later live out his days in California, where I now make my home.

My letter to Stuart was simple, and his reply was simpler still. Yet, it guided my life for the next 27 years. I wrote to him about how I had heard a call on my life to "full-time ministry." This is a phrase I try not to use anymore, but it was the only way in which I could communicate what God had said to me. I closed the letter by asking, "What is the best preparation for this call?" I know that I was expecting more detail than I received. His reply was so simple, yet profound in its capacity to define the course of my life: "Go and get experience working with people."

And so began a quest that would lead me to Psychiatric and General Nurse training at the London Hospital Whitechapel, famous to movie buffs for *The Elephant Man*. I loved nursing. Admittedly, there were highs and lows to the career, but nothing beats the high of saving a life, which was my privilege on the last day I worked as a nurse.

The decisions that have guided my career changes have not always been "spiritual," but sometimes very practical. My decision to leave nursing was for a necessary increase in income, as my wife was pregnant with our first son. However, when God is Lord of your life, He is Lord of all. He is a practical God. I often describe my life as a journey of watching for the arrows on the road, clues and confirmations from a God who speaks, not always in a still small voice.

My last day as a nurse was one such occasion of seeing the arrows on the road. I saved a man's life that day. That man worked in the Prison Service of England and Wales and was due to teach me the following week at the Prison Service College. His heart attack prevented that, but I still met him, as he lay on a table asystole (flat line). Giving him a firm thump, I watched the monitor return to sinus rhythm. As I saw life re-enter this man, who represented the next step in my journey, this was my confirmation that leaving a career I had trained for and loved was in His plan. Strangely, the other nurse on duty that day was raised in the U.S. and was a son of a prison manager. These were the only clues that I needed to confirm that God had ordained my next decision. These two coincidences pointing to the Prison Service would salve the pain of leaving my first love, nursing. Although my career move was pragmatic, I had God's hand firmly on it.

And so, I joined the Prison Service. Prison is an unlikely training ground for becoming a pastor. Or is it? Of course not, because it is all about people! Thank you Reverend Harris; you were right. I grew to love the Prison Service. It can be a grueling career, but I love changed lives, and I was privileged to see many lives change while I worked in prison. I will never forget standing on the back of a stage in Hyde Park at the annual Party in the Park. I was there because four young men in my prison had formed a band called The XKONZ, and they had successfully competed to perform in front of 100,000 people, including The Prince of Wales. My pride and joy that day caused me to walk past Elton John and not even notice the rock legend as those four young men and I left the stage on a high that we will never forget.

In 1997, after carrying a call to full-time ministry for 20 years, I stood on a street in Buenos Aires, Argentina, holding a fax informing me that I had been given my first in-charge position of a prison. I was to be a prison governor. As I stood there, Claudio Friesen came outside and stood with me. I was with a team from England that had been visiting him for a week. He asked what was in my hand, and I told him. Without any hesitation, he put his hands on my shoulders and looked me straight in the eyes. His words ring in my ears to this day, "Go back to England and run that prison for God."

Those words and his commissioning prayer changed my perspective toward having a call to ministry. I had been to dozens of meetings over the previous 20 years of waiting; dozens of altar calls to full-time ministry had passed me by, and now I heard my call in a new light—managing a prison. On my return from that trip to Argentina, I became, for the first time, content and able to fully embrace my call in the moment. That's not to say it was easy. There were challenges in our church life and family life, but I was able to move forward in the knowledge that I was no longer waiting for my destiny and call to happen to me. I was living it out every day.

In my last ten years in the prison service, I trained and spent much time developing and practicing skills in strategic planning. I led over 50 teams of prison officers through strategic planning workshops and had the pleasure of seeing them change their view of how to do their jobs. I watched as they came alive with ideas of how to better care for prisoners.

My experience of working for 19 years in the Prisons of England and Wales also exposed me to the ways of national government. When an organizational structure serves itself instead of the purpose for which it was formed, it becomes a bureaucracy. It is hard for government to avoid becoming bureaucratic, and yet its roots lie deep in the principles of ministry and servitude. Bureaucracy becomes the seedbed for a political spirit, which has one end, and that is division. How often we see that in the democratic governments of the world—men and women who have so much in common around a meal table, but when representing their own parties, they often divide.

Sadly these things are often true of the Church, as well. This organization, with a mandate from Heaven to be known for love and unity, is sadly more often known for division and protest. It is also often known for becoming a bureaucracy, failing over time to serve the purpose for which it was birthed and becoming a servant of its own structure, fighting to keep a relatively lifeless organization alive long after it has left the passionate conception of its founding fathers.

Around the same time I was developing strategic planning for prisons, I was studying a Senior Command course at Cambridge University in order to receive a Master of Studies degree. While at Cambridge, I read a book on Appreciative Inquiry that was written by one of my professors. The book discussed a model of management consultancy that focused on dreams, memories, stories and being appreciative. I scribbled in the margin of the book that this was "our" stuff, Kingdom principles being applied in the corporate and not-for-profit world.

Not long after this, I would listen to Bill Johnson expound on Revelation 19:10, "*...the testimony of Jesus is the spirit of prophecy.*" I immediately connected the dreams and memories of Appreciative Inquiry with prophecy and testimony and from there began to develop strategic planning workshops to help lead churches and other ministries into their destinies. I had been prepared in "Egypt," with the resources of Egypt, for a ministry that would eventually lead me around the world.

My background in strategic planning and the governmental training I received in Prison Management became the foundation for the wonderful task given to me in 2005 by Bill Johnson and Kris Vallotton. They asked me to build a worldwide network of revivalists. This network was not to host a political spirit, but it was to be a wineskin for one purpose: to carry the wine. The day they asked me, my spirit audibly said, "yes," and my head trembled. But for once, my spirit was leading. I looked at Bill and Kris and said, "I was born for this." Crazy statement. Crazy that a man with no seminary training, who had never led a church and never even made deacon, would believe he was born to build a network that would connect, resource, and encourage revival leaders around the world.

However, my Baptist neighbor had prophesied this very thing over me in the summer of 2001, just before I left England for California. At the end of a meeting, in which I shared my testimony, he began to prophesy that I would pastor pastors and lead leaders. At the time, it seemed an outrageous prophecy. I was going to California as a student, to attend the School of Supernatural Ministry.

My journey to Bethel actually began with my wife. She was led to come to Bethel and was the first in our family to make the journey to California to visit the church. My love for her and her courage to pursue God's plan caused us to change the course of our lives in our early 40s. God had prepared me to step into specific opportunities, which would in turn enable her to step into the destiny that God had ordained for her. He is an extraordinary God.

In 2001, my wife, our youngest son, and I reduced our lives to two suitcases each, a one-year visitor's visa, and enough money to live for three years. I had no expectation of being on staff at Bethel. At the least, I was hoping to get a job in probation or a prison or maybe retrain as a nurse. Yet, I had been prepared for what I would eventually find myself doing. It is, I believe, that two circumstances of life attract the lie of the enemy that "nothing has prepared me": unexpected promotion and crisis. The truth is, we are rarely unprepared. The real issue is not unpreparedness, but whether we have the ability to access the things that have prepared us.

In this context I nearly always think of Moses, a man who once stood before God and told Him that he was the wrong guy for the assigned task. Clearly he did not fully understand how uniquely he had been prepared his entire life. From being saved from genocide in a "Moses" basket and consequently raised in a palace, he became the only one of millions of traveling Israelites who would be able to interpret

God's description of the most extravagant worship center ever created. His familiarity with the palace life and the complex features of that life enabled him to listen to the instructions from God during those incredible 40 days on top of the mountain and then bring the detail back down to the wilderness and administrate the construction of the tabernacle.

The 40 years Moses spent looking after his father-in-law's sheep prepared him to "shepherd" an entire nation out of slavery and into freedom. It also, I believe, created a relationship that would later be a source of wisdom for Moses. When he was overwhelmed by the requests of his people, Moses was advised by his father-in-law on how to build an organizational structure that would enable the people to hear God, but without Moses continuing to exhaust himself.

Despite mistakes of grabbing his destiny too early and misunderstanding what he was to do, Moses was called, guided, and prepared. Still, he can be mistaken as a man who missed his calling by not making it into the Promised Land. However, not only did he make it into the Promised Land, but on the top of the mount of transfiguration, he received the complete answer to his audacious request of God to show him His glory. Just when you think you may have missed it or you are not prepared, remind yourself of Moses and you may just be inspired. Unique preparation has been a part of my life and is likely to be a part of yours as well.

God wastes nothing, and He is the instigator and motivator of our preparation. Each of us is unique, and as we come to embrace our preparation, He is able to lead us into the next level of Kingdom impact.

As my experience has shown me, a call from the Lord is perhaps better defined as an invitation to a journey, rather than a destination. As I continue my own journey, I am aware that God wastes nothing. I left my health care career over 30 years ago, and yet, today I get to minister to health care professionals and encourage them in their careers as ministers of the Gospel of the Kingdom, whether they minister by surgical or medical skill or supernatural power. The same is true of my career in criminal justice, as I recently spoke in the UK about how the Kingdom could help solve the issues of gang and youth crime on the streets of my beloved London.

Don't give up on your journey. Learning to embrace your "call" in everything you do, no matter where you find yourself, may be the greatest reward. The pursuit of a journey and choosing to resist the temptation to camp out where you are is a key to understanding that there are no limits to what God can do with a life submitted. Called, guided, and prepared. Trust me, I could not have planned this journey in a dozen lifetimes.

Destiny is rarely fully revealed in a moment or achieved in one step. It is most often a marvelous interplay of who we are, what we are here for, and where we are headed.

If your life is anything like mine, there will be twists and turns, some of which will be ordained by Him and some redeemed or re-crafted by Him to fulfill His plans. Make Him Lord of All. Trust your call, watch for the guideposts, and believe that you are fully prepared for each new step or promotion along the way.

Chapter 8

SHOULD I BUY BREAD? SHOULD I WEAR RED?... WHAT'S THAT GOD SAID?

by Pam Spinosi

Should I buy bread?
Should I wear red?
Sleep on a stone or
Pillow my head?
Is it OK to buy a bed?
Should I turn left?
Should I turn right?
Drive down the road
To lighten my load?

Or must I toil all night?
Should I deny?
Should I reply?
Should I just hide
And not decide?
In all these things I have to die.
Should I spend, or must I save?
Pray and rest, or work and slave?
Live by faith or be employed?
Somber, staid or overjoyed?
Leave my hopes in the grave?
Should I ignore my heart and soul?
Should I be part? May I be whole?
Lay down my plans for how to live?
Concentrate on how to give?
Will I ever find my role?

***

"Do you have a call to the nations?" the visiting minister asked.

"Well, I, uh, I *desire* to go to the nations, but then I always have, so I don't know if it's God, but I, well, I do hope to, but only if, you know, um...."

Before I could spit out my answer, the minister had slipped past me to the next person, maybe one who could answer yes or no to a simple question.

The truth was that I did have a call to the nations, but at 16, I was so blinded by teaching that I had received about God's will that I couldn't tell. I had been born again for a year and had left the worldly lifestyle and lifeless church I had been in and landed in a church that embraced the Gospel and the gifts of the Spirit and had a love for the Word and an earnest desire to please God. But my new church enjoyed those graces alongside a very narrow view of the Christian life.

The formative years of my Christian walk took place during the height of the Jesus Movement and the Charismatic Renewal. To come to the Lord then was easy. We young people fell like very ripe fruit right into the waiting arms of our Savior. The satisfaction we couldn't find in thrills, strange Eastern religions, and psychedelic drugs, we found in Him. I gladly let go of everything when I found out my lifelong desire to know God was possible. My mother marveled as the daughter who only wanted to party with her friends now spent hours in Bible reading and prayer. In my first two years as a Christian, I experienced great waves of God's presence and began an intimate walk with Him, nourished by the words of classic Christian authors like Hannah Hurnard, Andrew Murray, and Watchman Nee.

In my bliss, I didn't notice the incongruence between the loving God I was coming to know and the stern picture of Him painted by some people in my church. They would say things to me like, "Oh, don't ask to see angels. You'll get deceived." "Those wonderful feelings you are having of God's presence, they'll go away. That doesn't last."

Following my week at youth camp, I returned home smelly and with dirty hair (we'd run out of water and couldn't shower the last couple of days), wearing no makeup, and wearing a long, borrowed dress that could not have ever been in style in any decade. My mother opened the door, and I stuck a fist in the air and shouted, "Hallelujah!" Then I ran through the house, discarding everything I'd just been taught was evil: the record albums, makeup, cards, and any pair of jeans I could find. Helped by a move to California a few years later, I eventually chilled out about all that—mostly. But what had a lasting and more sinister effect on my walk with God were the views of His will that I had developed, views that would cripple my ability to make decisions or follow the course for my life for years to come.

Some of the Christians around me were fond of admonishing, "You had better never say that you don't want to go to Africa because that is just where God will send you." From their talk, I got the impression that God and I were never going to want the same thing or be on the same page. I lived in dread of being asked to marry someone I didn't love and began to have nightmares about it. I think I watched two friends do just that; they believed it was God's will. I prayed about every tiny thing and feared making a mistake. Today I recognize that that sort of fear is never from God. Fear is never an indication that you are on the right path. But back then I didn't realize the bind I was in. I love the true fear of God, but that is another thing altogether. The true fear of God bears good fruit in our lives. The fear I had did not.

My friend from church made a big point of her sacrifice of her artistic talents for her own call to the mission field, and she was the primary influence in my decision to quit ballet, something I had been doing since I was 4, something I was really good at. My church didn't think it was godly, and after about a year, I let it go.

I started making straight A's again because I wanted to please God by doing my best and because I genuinely loved to learn. I believe that when we come to Jesus, we are freed to be who we really are, not what we were trying to be to please people. Before I started changing out of peer pressure, I had been a straight-A student who loved to learn. Now a Christian, I found the desire and discipline to study well again. I had a desire to go to college, but I also had a longing for full-time ministry. I couldn't see how the two could go together, but I really wanted an education. I had an appointment to see a counselor at an excellent university, probably the best university in my area. But when my friend from Christian school and I stepped foot on campus, we were "weirded" out by some of the sights we saw and the dress and behavior of the students. We didn't even keep our appointment.

We fled. I had somehow learned to fear the world, not to invade it with the truth.

Because of my indecision, I did not apply on time for any other school and ended up spending the next two years at my local community college, which wasn't fun or challenging for me. Each semester, I would go through my ritual of asking if it was OK to still be in college and stressing over which classes to take. I had always heard people talk about hearing God's voice in a way that made me think I never heard it. I somehow thought He spoke to other people in long discourses. But I didn't get those, so I thought I couldn't hear Him. I also never considered that, in His love, He was more interested in guiding me than I was in receiving guidance. Thus, I experienced striving and turmoil every time I had to make a decision.

The fourth year into my Christian life, I moved to California with my widowed mother to be nearer to my sister, who had married and moved out here and was pregnant with her second child. California was a place of great beauty and freedom for me. Moving here broke the lie that I would be stuck in the little town I grew up in forever even though I longed to see the world. I still struggled every semester with the question of whether to go to college—until one day when I received a verse that showed me my folly. I was seriously thinking of dropping out of college to attend a Bible school on a mountain in another state. As I was reading, I felt God had highlighted Psalm 11:1 to me, *"In the Lord put I my trust. How say ye to my soul, flee as a bird to your mountain?"* (KJV). I understood with a chuckle that I had wanted to go there merely to escape. I was so afraid of the world and its influence. But God was showing me that it was OK to stay in college. So I settled in and allowed myself to get first my B.A. and then my M.A. in English.

But I found other things to exercise my guidance bondage over. First, it was the Russian language. I had had a longing to go to Russia ever since I became a Christian. (I wonder who put *that* there?) My desire increased so much that I decided to take a Russian class. But something kept telling me I should drop my Russian class. I had such a sense of dread. Why I associated feelings like that with the Lord, I don't know, but sometimes I did. Finally, on the last day to add or drop, a Friday, I dropped my Russian class. But I didn't feel better. I was still miserable. "I don't understand, Lord," I said. "I thought You wanted me to drop it. Why do I still feel bad?" I had expected relief. I sought the Lord about it.

That evening, at the home Bible study I attended, the leader had us pray for Russia, something we had not done before. As we were in a circle praying, he prophesied, "Someone in this room is going to Russia! Claim this Scripture: 'Touch not mine anointed, and do my prophets no harm.'" That was during the Cold War days when Americans couldn't easily jump up and go to Russia. The leader kept on the subject for a while, strongly asserting that someone in the room was going there. I knew I was the one. *Who else could it be?*

"I wonder what they eat in Russia?" he mused.

"Borscht!" I said. I held that prophetic word in my heart and popped my head into my Russian professor's office on Monday morning, "Is there any way you could let me back into class?" He did, and I made mostly A's for the next five semesters.

And everyone I knew started giving me Russian books. They'd see a Russian book and buy it for me. I was the person they knew studying Russian. One of the books was a Russian Bible with the inscription, "May the Lord use you and this Bible to minister to the Russian-speaking people of the world." I gave that Bible to the Russian taxi driver I led to the Lord the year I moved to the Soviet Union.

A more critical guidance crisis came as I was nearing graduation with my Master's degree. I was offered a teaching position in Japan. That was a curveball for me, for I had not been considering going to Japan. I was planning to go to Finland, where a relative had contacts for me and from which I could go with others to Russia. I was excited about it. But when the invitation to Japan came, my sensible brother-in-law advised me to consider that wonderful opportunity. I didn't know what to do, so I sought God for guidance. I fasted, prayed, struggled, and strove. I was so preoccupied that I once left a Malaysian student in the hall for the entire class period. He was only supposed to stay out five minutes until we finished going over the test he had missed and would be making up. I felt so bad about that. I felt good, though, about the weight I'd lost through the whole process. But I wanted a word from God, a clear direction, and He only seemed to be saying one thing to me: "Do it by faith." *Do what by faith? Tell me what to do, and I'll do it by faith!* Why was He so hard to figure out?

In the end, I didn't go to Japan. I didn't go to Finland, either. I ended up back in my home state, in another church that seemed to be so exciting, but wound up going into error. I was working there and couldn't seem to get free of the place. I thought it was God's will for me. My heart was overseas, but I thought God had me there. Through a friend and perhaps the many prayers of others who could see I was trapped in the wrong place, I finally rose up and moved to Washington, D.C. That move marked the first time I had gone to a place merely because I wanted to live there. My sister's friend prophesied over me that God was going to use that move in my life to give me greater authority and independence. Washington was pivotal for me. There God healed me of the damages done by the last few years. Also, I began to prepare for my life abroad.

One day in 1989, almost in my third year in Washington, I cried out to the Lord in my living room, "Lord the [Berlin] Wall is down! Things are warming up in Russia. Why aren't I there? Please send me!" Shortly after, I found out about a private college in

Tallinn, Estonia, that was hiring teachers. That was close enough to Russia for me. On the weekend when I said to God, "Lord, I have to know this weekend if I am going to go because I have to give notice at my job and at my apartment," a couple who ministered in Estonia landed at our church because they had thought there would be a visiting minister there— but there wasn't. Meeting them seemed like a divine appointment, and knowing they would be in Estonia, too, was encouraging. I took it all as a sign and took the teaching job in Tallinn.

I ended up only teaching there one semester. For the next few months, I traveled around the Soviet Union with missionaries. On one such trip, sitting in a busload of Finns chattering around me in Finnish, I was reflecting on all that I had experienced in those months, and I felt that the "soldiers" of doubt of my call had been drowned in the Red Sea. No longer would I doubt my call to the nations. There was no going back.

Another thing happened in that time period. While I was still in Washington, the Lord seemed to lead me back to dance. What had died, been buried, and had a tombstone on it was being resurrected by Him. One of the ways I ministered in the Soviet Union was in dance. I did not have the skill I would have had if I had kept it up, but I still had a lot of form and beauty to my dance, and God was anointing it. I would for the next decade and a half, train again and enjoy a wonderful dance ministry in three nations (with short jaunts in 15 nations, altogether).

Near the end of my time there, while on one of my journeys to the Ukraine, I was seized with a strong desire to go to Israel. I said, "Lord, I want to see Your land." But I had phoned my mother before embarking on that trip and asked her to purchase my ticket to go home with money that I had there. I had no way of contacting her to ask her not to buy the ticket. In those days, a call to America had to be ordered two weeks in advance in the Ukraine. I would have to wait a few days until I got back to Tallinn to call her. When I got back, I phoned her and asked if she had bought my ticket. She said no. I asked her why not, and she said that she had felt she needed to wait until she heard from me again. I felt the Lord's presence for the next two days: I was going to Israel.

My month in Israel was like a honeymoon. I spent it falling in love with Jerusalem and meeting all kinds of interesting people: Jews, Arabs, missionaries, Christian pilgrims from all over the world, Sephardic Jews with tales to tell, seeking Messianic Jews from the UK and Russia considering *Aliyah* (emigration to Israel). I would have gladly moved there, but I knew it wasn't the time yet. I went back to the States and worked for a few months. Then I ran out of work and money and needed a vision. The only thing I had at that point was a desire to move to Finland. I'd made lots of trips there while I was in Estonia and experienced what I believe was a call there while listening to a tape of Kent Henry singing, "I Have a Destiny" on my first trip to Finland en route to Estonia. I'd also had a dream that I believe was about Finland before I had ever set foot there.

I wrote some letters of inquiry. I asked a lady how much the empty apartment she owned in Helsinki would cost. She wrote back, "I just asked God today what to do with that apartment. Then I got your letter. You can stay there for free until you find work." That was enough for me. Jobless, penniless, and helpless, I announced, "I'm going to Finland." No one around me believed me. But as soon as I said that, things got into motion. I received enough temporary work over the next three months to purchase a round-trip ticket to Finland, attend a teacher's conference in Vancouver on the way, and leave with $300 in my pocket. My confirmation that time was at my friend, Jane's, house in Washington, D.C., on my way there. She put cardamom in my tea. No one ever does that in the States, do they? Cardamom reminds me of Finland more than anything else; they put it in their pastries and, at Christmas, in their coffee. On my flight there, I was seated next to American missionaries to Iceland, and we had wonderful fellowship all the way over. All confirmations.

The crowning moment for me was the ferry ride from Sweden to Finland. I had paid for half of a shared cabin, but I had it all to myself. I'll never forget the joy and tranquility of the night ride floating in that ferry. I was sublimely happy, knowing that I was fulfilling a great desire, but assured that it was truly *God's* desire, too. Those three months in Helsinki were a glorious time of seeing God provide everything I needed—even a job. I went back at the end of my three months, got my work visa, and returned to teach English, minister in dance, and be an active part of a church and a Christian school for nearly five years.

Those were the years I learned a new thing: being led by my *desires*. I would get a desire to go to a country, and a year later, I would be there. Six months after I tried to spend Christmas in France (I felt that the Lord had said no), I got to go there with Youth With A Mission's Summer of Service program. While in France, I developed a desire to go to North Africa. The next summer found me on a prayer trip to Tunisia with YWAMers—paid for entirely by a bundle of money dropped in my backpack at church. I had the joy of going back to Israel two more times—both, I'm sure, in the timing of the Lord. I had the delight of going to many other places in that season.

In all this, I've learned a valuable lesson. The result of my fearful efforts *not* to miss God's will was that I had done little else *but* miss it! When I began to understand that He has many ways to speak to us, I relaxed and heard Him in new ways or at least began to recognize His voice in ways I had not before. One of the main new ways I learned was through my desires. When my heart would long to go to a place, I found that if I moved in that direction, either of two things would happen: 1) He would shut the door by removing my peace or by some other means or 2) He would open the door. I'd take it as a green light and see it unfold as I moved ahead. I've found I hear "no" more loudly than I hear "go," so I have made "go" my default. As I head that way, He is faithful to show me if I am off the path. I've learned to trust Him as the good God that He is, who delights to bless His children. He made me to love the nations, not so I would pine away, staring at postcards, but so I could *go*. He brought back dance into my life and blessed the ministry that I had in dance for a very long season. Though I've laid my teaching career down many times, He's blessed it as well.

I realize, too, that God speaks to me in other ways: pictures in my mind, impressions, feelings, and yes, the occasional English words that I'd wanted all along. Usually, His words to me are few, but they get my attention. He can change the way He wants to speak at any time.

I was so relieved when I came to Bethel and heard a message about God's green light and our sanctified desires. Here I heard that God has made His will known to us—heal the sick, raise the dead, release the captives—and that many of the other choices, unless God specifically tells us otherwise, are optional. If my gift is evangelism, it will manifest no matter what I'm doing, even when I'm shopping. I began to notice that the apostle Paul didn't always have to have a specific word to go somewhere. Sometimes He did, like the Macedonian call he received through a vision. But other times, he would announce that he was going to go check on the churches to see how they were doing. He knew his calling, and he operated in a green light except for the explicit occasions when God warned him otherwise, and that He did very clearly.

What I want to say in all this is *live. Choose. Act. Go!* If you don't know what to do, ask yourself what brings you life, fills you with joy, gets you into the Lord's presence. What is His blessing on in your life? Those are good indications of what you were born to do. Follow the direction of your desires, knowing that God will put up roadblocks (even if only a warning removal of peace) if you are not heading in a good way, and He will open doors and provide for you in wonderful ways if you are. Life is a dance, and God is one of the partners in it; you are the other. Dance with Him into the fulfillment of your purpose, making choices together, co-laboring. Live fully and intentionally in the unique place in His Body reserved just for you.

Chapter 9

LIVING IN REST
by Crystal Stiles

The foundation of living in rest is trusting the heart of our Father. We can't rest if we don't trust. The story of the Israelites' long path into the Promised Land is the ultimate picture of rest. Hebrews 3:19 says they were kept out because of their unbelief. Did they not believe that the land existed? No, they actually spied out the land and saw the beauty of its fruit and abundance. I think their unbelief was directed at God's heart; they did not believe in the goodness and commitment of the One who had made the promise to lead them and keep them. The Israelites couldn't enter their rest because they kept wavering in their trust of the Father. They often turned to their own strength or other gods and stopped looking to the One who is faithful.

The enemy's greatest scheme from the very beginning was to drive a wedge between us and the Father, inviting Adam and Eve to question God's command and ultimately the intention of His heart. The serpent's goal was to steal our place of intimacy and oneness. The Father has such a desire to lead us back into His rest—the place of total intimacy, acceptance, love, and favor. I think it is His greatest passion to restore us to the place we had in the garden before separation from His heart began.

My journey into the land of rest has been a series of different encounters with the Lord, whispers from His heart, or Scriptures that jumped out and grabbed me. Maybe I'm a slow learner or maybe it's because this is my life message, but I seem to need continued revelation about remaining in this place of rest and dusting off traces of "Egyptian" soil that somehow follow me into my Promised Land.

As the Israelites entered their Promised Land, they were commanded to take 12 stones from the Jordan and build a memorial to serve as a sign for future generations. I hope my altar of stones speaks to you of the love and acceptance of your Father. As you read about my revelation, I pray that you will have your own.

A Garden Encounter

My journey began with a dream and ended with a vision. I call this my Garden Encounter, and it was probably one of the most profound "memorial stone" experiences of my life.

One night I had a dream:

I was hanging on a cross (yes, a big wooden one). It was night, and I was in my bedroom, and my father was sleeping in the room next door. I felt that my father wanted me to be on this cross. However, I was handed a key and an opportunity to get off, and I took it! I snuck off the cross and went out into my backyard. It was edged by an orchard of trees. I loved it. I felt so full of life, like I was truly breathing for the first time. It was so wonderful that I decided to concoct a plan.

I would hide the key and then every day when my father left for work, I would sneak off the cross and enjoy the garden. When my father came home, I'd make sure I was back on the cross to greet him, the perfect picture of the obedient child, right?

As I was thinking of my plan, I suddenly realized morning had come, and my father was leaving for work. I did not have time to make it back to the cross. In a panic, I crouched next to a bush, trying to hide as he walked by. I looked into his face. What would he think when he saw me off of the cross? What were his feelings toward me? But as he looked at me, it was as if he looked past me, and I couldn't tell what he felt. His face was blank.

This was the end of my dream. I felt troubled. What did it mean? Why didn't I know how my father felt about me? Why was I trying to hide from him? Over the next few months, I would periodically bring the dream up in prayer and ask the Lord about it. I had a feeling that the Lord would bring me another dream or give me an encounter in some way to fully explain what He was trying to show me. So I waited.

A Picture of My True Father

Months later, I had a vision. It was not an open vision, but rather one where I was walking through a picture in my mind. However the picture came to me, it wasn't something that I was trying to imagine. This time I found myself standing in an orchard of trees.

This is the orchard from my dream, I thought. As I stood in the orchard, I saw a Gardener walking down a row of trees. He was watering each one with a watering can. And He was looking into my eyes. His eyes were so beautiful, full of love, acceptance, and affection. If eyes could smile, His did. I knew that this Gardener was my true Father, that this was my orchard, and that I was meant to live here always. He was in the place that I had felt most alive in my dream, most full of breath. He lived in the garden of my delight, and I was meant to live there, too. He began to tell me things that He liked about who I was—little things from my childhood. He also told me that He was my biggest cheerleader and that I could have as much fruit as I wanted.

In this vision, I saw the heart of my Father, my beautiful Gardener. This encounter connects to John 15:1-5. Jesus says:

> *I am the true vine, and My Father is the gardener. He cuts off every branch in Me that bears no fruit, while every branch that does bear fruit He prunes so that it will be even more fruitful. You are already clean because of the word I have spoken to you. Remain in Me, and I will remain in you. No branch can bear fruit by itself; it must remain in the vine. Neither can you bear fruit unless you remain in Me. I am the vine; you are the branches. If you remains in Me and I in you, you will bear much fruit; apart from Me you can do nothing* (NIV).

The Father is our Gardener. He is caring for us—for our orchard. The person in my first dream was not a true father. He was an image of a religious god that I had been trying to live up to my whole life. He worked hard and expected a lot out of me. It was about sacrifice and serving in order to try to keep him pleased. I was trying to impress him with my behavior. But I could never really be sure of how he felt about me. Just as Adam and Eve had been tempted to view a father who was holding out on them, in my dream I felt that I, too, was missing out and needed to sneak around in order to have access to the garden.

In contrast, my true Father, the Gardener, actually lived in the place where I felt the most alive and the most free. The place that I loved the most was the place where He dwelt and where I was meant to dwell. The garden that I felt was too good to be true, where I was almost guilty in my enjoyment, was the place where He met me and gave me permission to be. He was not trying to keep something good from me, but actually wanted me to live in this land of more than I could ever ask or imagine.

Living with the Gardener

You have permission to live in the garden. Jesus died on the cross so that you would have access to His provision. It is important to Him that you are living in the fullness of His joy (see John 15:11). Your Gardener is waiting out there for you to join Him. Don't be afraid. There is no need to hide. He wants to help you breathe the air of His grace and acceptance. Is your breathing restricted? That is what happens when you hang on a cross. Your air supply is slowly cut off. If you try to perform for what He already paid for, you can't truly breathe, and you aren't fully alive.

While I was jumping on and off crosses and worrying about His approval, the Father was peacefully out in my garden, watering my trees and tending to the fruit on my branches. There is a simple point here: He is the Gardener, not me. Many of us have picked up our gardening tools and pulled on our overalls and are trudging around trying to make sure we are producing fruit. We are working very hard to produce a good crop. But John 15 says that the Father is the Gardener. Our job is to be the branch.

After I had my dream and vision, I discovered a passage in Deuteronomy. The Israelites were being instructed regarding entering their Promised Land—their place of rest. In Deuteronomy 11:10-12, Moses instructs them:

> *The land you are entering to take over is not like the land of Egypt, from which you have come, where you planted your seed and irrigated it by foot as in a vegetable garden. But the land you are crossing the Jordan to take possession of is a land of mountains and valleys that drinks rain from heaven. It is a land the Lord your God cares for; the eyes of the Lord your God are continually on it from the beginning of the year to its end* (NIV).

When we don the gardening clothes and feel that we are ultimately responsible for cultivating our garden and making sure we produce, we are living in bondage, not the land of His rest. The Lord wants to be the Gardener in our lives. He wants us to live in full expectation of His provision and continual care. We are to live from His supernatural resources (rain from Heaven), not the irrigation ditches of our own sweat and toil. I know that we are also called to partner with Him and make good decisions, but if we do not first understand His commitment to care for us and His total acceptance of us, we will end up striving to produce what is meant to be a natural bi-product of simply abiding in Him.

Understanding His Love and Pleasure

My Gardener told me He was my biggest cheer-leader. This one little phrase says so much about who the Father wants to be in our lives. He is totally for us, totally committed. He is the one standing on the sidelines, yelling out our names. "You can do it! I believe in you! You are going to win!"

His Word is full of reminders of His feelings toward us—more memorial stones I've pocketed on my journey. I love Romans 8:31-32:

> *What, then, shall we say in response to this? If God is for us, who can be against us? He who did not spare His own Son, but gave Him up for us all—how will He not also, along with Him, graciously give us all things?* (NIV)

And Isaiah 30:18 says,

"Yet the Lord longs to be gracious to you; He rises to show you compassion. For the Lord is a God of justice. Blessed are all who wait for Him" (NIV).

There He is again, our wonderful Cheerleader, rising up out of His seat, like an excited fan in the last play of the game. He is rising to show us compassion. At present, we are in the last play of the game. The Father and the cloud of witnesses are all cheering us on. What we sometimes fail to realize is that we are simply running the victory lap of the race that Jesus already won. We are fully accepted sons and daughters running and abiding in the finished work of the cross.

Recently, the Lord again expanded my view of His nature. I have a spiritual mom in my life who is kind and understanding toward me, even in my weakness. She believes in me and wants the best for me. She enjoys me. When I make a mistake, she is the first person I want to tell because I know she will both hold me to a standard of greatness and offer me grace in my humanness as well. I am confident in her affection and love. God began to whisper to my heart, "You sometimes expect more from Debbie than you do from Me. Don't you think that I will be as kind to you as she would?" He reminded me of Matthew 7:9-11:

Which of you, if his son asks for bread, will give him a stone? Or if he asks for a fish, will give him a snake? If you, then, though you are evil, know how to give good gifts to your children, how much more will your Father in heaven give good gifts to those who ask Him? (NIV)

If Debbie in her humanness can love so well, how much more should I expect of my heavenly Father? As He spoke to me, I realized that it hurts His heart when I don't expect enough out of Him and when I don't perceive Him rightly. He was beckoning me to come into His perfect love, and He was enlarging my perception of His true identity.

Knowing His Voice

The enemy is called the accuser of the brethren (see Rev. 12:10-11). Sometimes I get tricked into listening to his voice, thinking it is the Father. I hear things like "You need to try harder. You aren't doing enough…" and so on. I somehow think that listening to those words will motivate me to be more fruitful. However, I find that it actually stunts my growth and causes me to hide from God. I end up running from the only One who has the grace and strength that I need.

When we are listening to the wrong voice, we often entertain the wrong question. We hear the accuser whisper, "Is He pleased with you?" But the Gardener is asking us, "Are you fully abiding in My pleasure?"

A while back I heard the Lord say, "Let the words of My affection drown out the voice of the accuser." As the Gardener met me in my orchard, He told me what He loved about me. I felt His pleasure wash over me. Hearing His words of affection helps to silence the enemy's voice. When I start to feel tempted to listen to accusation, I have learned to run into the arms of my Gardener instead. The tone of our Father's voice carries love and grace. He is always inviting us into deeper connection. As we listen for the Father, we must make sure we recognize this tone; if we don't, it is time to check the source.

No Longer a Slave

In John 15:15, Jesus says He no longer wants us as slaves. He wants us as His friends. When we don't know our true Father, however, we continue in slavery instead. We try to work for someone who says that we are His workmanship (see Eph. 2:10). We want to be seen and approved by someone who has already hidden us deep in the center of His heart (see Col. 3:3). He has taken us into the center of who He is and made us a part of His being, His very DNA. A branch is an extension of the vine, made of the same DNA. The branch's only job is to stay connected, dependent, one. The natural by-product will be fruit. Any other method by which a branch would produce fruit would be artificial, pharisaical in nature.

Because I often felt I needed to behave my way into favor, my ability to receive love and acceptance was always dependent on my behavior for the day. This left me striving for something that was already mine. In other words, I was living on a cross in my bedroom, working in a room that should have been my place of rest.

The Israelites often found themselves here as well. Isaiah 30:15 says, *"In repentance and rest is your salvation, in quietness and trust is your strength, but you would have none of it"* (NIV). The passage goes on to tell of the Israelites' plan to save themselves with swift horses and how the Lord knew that it would not work. Sometimes the Lord will let us strive in our own strength until we get tired enough to receive from His. He watches us struggling to perform for His love, trying to "save" ourselves with our behavior. Yet He longs to be gracious to us (see Isa. 30:18). It is not His grace that is lacking or His help that is not coming to me. It is just that I have often been too busy saddling up the horse of my own strength, working as a self-driven slave, in order to prove to Him how able I am to be worthy of His love.

I can almost hear the words of Paul speaking to my heart, "Oh you foolish Galatians! After beginning with the Spirit, are you now trying to attain your goal by human effort?" (Gal. 3:1,3, my paraphrase). Our Gardener is asking the same thing. "Do you really think you will start with grace and finish with striving?"

Grace Triumphs Over Guilt

How many of you have said, "I should have it together. I should know this by now." I think we often feel guilty for needing His help. However, the truth is that our dependence is what pleases Him. The nature of a branch is that it is nothing without the vine. When we start to feel the need to impress our Father, we must just press deeper into our connection in the vine. We aren't supposed to be able to do this thing called Christianity without Him. That is just a term that we have made up, anyway. It's not even in the Bible. We are not supposed to do Christianity; we are supposed to be. Be a branch, be a friend, be a son, be a daughter.

I also love the passage in Isaiah 50:10-11. It may not seem like it, but this is a really encouraging passage.

Who among you fears the Lord and obeys the word of His servant? Let him who walks in the dark, who has no light, trust in the name of the Lord and rely on his God. But now, all of you who light fires and provide yourselves with flaming torches, go, walk in the light of your fires and the torches you have set ablaze. This is what you shall receive from my hand: you will lie down in torment (NIV).

In these verses, we are given permission to depend on His grace and stop trying to do "it" ourselves. We must not live by the light of our own fires, but admit we are in desperate need of His. God likes that. It pleases Him for us to need Him, to not be able to make it without Him. It is interesting that, in this passage, the only source of torment came because they were trying to light their own fire instead of receiving His. When we operate out of striving and produce out of our own strength, we open the door to the tormentor.

I shared my dream and encounter with a group of students, preaching the message of the Father. A week later, I had a dream that the sound department came and gave me a CD of my message. They had entitled it, "Symposium of Grace." I love when I don't really know what a word means, because I figure God must be speaking. I looked up the word *symposium* and found out it originated from the Greek. In Greece, the men would gather together, drink wine, and discuss ideas. One definition of *symposium* is a "drinking party." We are called to live in a constant drinking party of His grace. We are meant to be filled with the knowledge of His acceptance, favor, and absolute goodness toward us.

The Father is so passionate for us. He so longs to have us stay in the garden with Him always. Just as His heart broke when Adam and Eve were hiding from Him, His heart breaks when we hide from His love, thinking that we are only presentable in the fig leaves of our performance. He is coming after us with a vengeance. His love is going to chase us down. He will not relent until we know the fullness of His heart. In light of this dream and encounter, let's read the following passage and see the passion of the Father who is fighting for our intimacy:

In that day, the Lord will punish with His sword, His fierce, great and powerful sword, Leviathan the gliding serpent, Leviathan the coiling serpent; He will slay the monster of the sea. In that day—"Sing about a fruitful vineyard: I, the Lord, watch over it; I water it continually. I guard it day and night so that no one may harm it. I am not angry. If only there were briers and thorns confronting Me! I would march against them in battle; I would set them all on fire. Or else let them come to Me for refuge; let them make peace with Me, yes, let them make peace with Me." In days to come Jacob will take root, Israel will bud and blossom and fill all the world with fruit (Isaiah 27:1-6 NIV).

God is coming to punish someone, but it is not us! It is the enemy of our souls—the serpent. It is so important for us to hear Him emphatically say, "I am not angry." That is His constant, everyday stance with us. His anger was taken care of on the cross. He found a way to make peace with us through Jesus. We are living "In that day…." The Gardener is singing about His vineyard, and we are His beautiful branches.

Prayer to Your Gardener

As you look at this altar that I have built, my memorial stones regarding the goodness of the Father, I want to invite you to encounter His love and acceptance in a new way. Take a drink of His grace and feel free to pray this prayer to your Gardener:

Dear Gardener,

Forgive me for making You less than You truly are. Forgive me for letting the enemy steal my intimacy. Forgive me for trying to earn Your love by wearing fig leaves of performance.

I want to enter Your rest. I accept my assignment as Your branch and receive permission to be fully dependent on You.

Thank You, Lord, that You are coming to crush the serpent who has tried to steal our connection.

Thank You that You are not angry. Thank You that You are marching out on my behalf. Thank You that You want me to be at peace with You, at home with You. Thank You that You are my biggest cheerleader and my greatest support. Thank You that You are watching over my vineyard.

You guard me day and night so nothing will harm me. Thank You that I will fill the world with fruit.

Amen.

After Words

Below is a poem I wrote to the Gardener about the house in my first dream. It is a great way to ponder where you are at in your journey toward rest. If you find yourself in the wrong house as you read, don't be discouraged. Just shake the dust off your feet and keep going on your pilgrimage into His heart.

House of Religion

When You become something I'm trying to
live up to rather than someone I'm living with,

I've moved into the house of religion.

When I'm considering my Christianity
and measuring its status,

I've moved into the house of religion.

When I talk about You more than I speak with You,

I've moved into the house of religion.

When I think of my actions, wondering if You're
pleased, but forgetting that You know my thoughts,

I've moved into the house of religion.

When I forget that You hold my hand, dream
with me at night, wake me up in the morning,

I've moved into the house of religion.

Let's find our way back to Eden.

Let's find our way back to time
without fear of wasting it,

love without fear of losing it,

life without knowing the end of it.

Let's find our way back to the beginning when
You created just for the sake of being with me.

I'm sorry I locked myself out today, relegated myself
to wishing and sighing, moaning and dying.

Waiting for Your disappointment
rather than basking in Your approval.

I'm sorry that somehow I went to the wrong
address, the door was open, and I walked right in.

It all looked so familiar,
like a place I once knew, but forgot.

I moved back to the house of religion,
but all my stuff is still in the garden of truth.

I think I'll go back; I can get there quicker
than this thought. It's only a drop away.

Because Your blood does speak a better word!

Chapter 10

CELEBRATE THE SIMPLE
by Bill Johnson

Here is a synopsis of a few themes covered by Bill Johnson in Question and Answer sessions with third-year interns at the Bethel School of Supernatural Ministry.

New Wineskins

What does church look like?

Joy Over God's Presence—*Wineskins* are not the treasure. The *wine* (God's presence) is always the treasure. If you keep the treasure (God's presence) in mind, you will automatically build something that holds the treasure.

Celebration of People—Whether you are with 1,000 or 10, value the presence of God on others. Celebrate the people around you and value the grace on them. Call out who they are and the strengths that are in them.

Invading the Impossible—Confront things that will leave, not because of who you are, but because of who *He* is. You want to have a church life that requires you to change, or you will become ingrown. You want something exploding; you want to do things you could not do without the power of God. The thing that God is doing must drive what is going on.

If you have all those things, and they are increasing, you will have a government that holds new wineskins. These are the three elements to give attention to. Keep those three things in mind, even if you are just leading a cell group.

The Spiritual and the Secular

The Lord doesn't have a life of natural and supernatural. He only has a life of supernatural, which is natural. There is no line. The more you are able to erase the line between sacred and secular, the more effective you will be in living your life, because you don't have to turn on ministry.

If the Lord drops 1,000 dollars out of the air or someone gives me the opportunity to earn it, both are supernatural. One is harder to celebrate because it's possible for me to take credit for it. *"The horse is prepared for the day of battle, but victory belongs to the Lord"* (Prov. 21:31 NASB). It's hard to pour out effort and not take credit. We have to say, "God, it's only by grace." Even if you did everything right in raising your kids, you still have to say, "It's only by the grace of God."

If you learn how to blur the line between sacred and secular well, you'll represent the Gospel more effectively in all different fields.

Hiddenness

Celebrate hiddenness. The Lord increases the anointing on your life in secret, and He allows a few to see it. You only know who you are when no one is watching your decisions. Can you live with who you are when nobody knows what you do in secret? Then can you be trusted with favor when people celebrate you? Can you be entrusted with praise as God slowly removes the curtain that has kept you hidden? With favor and the right opportunity, you will influence nations.

Do not seek to be unhidden. Treasure being hidden. When the Lord unveils you, celebrate it. Look for chances to be hidden. If my name is mentioned, I give thanks for the honor of being mentioned. If my name is not mentioned, I celebrate being hidden.

Rest

Your free time is never wasted unless you pour into something that drains your life or denies who you are, for example, if people watch television programs that contradict who they are or their values. If it's recreational, rejuvenating, then it's not a waste of time. That's the simple life that I value. It contributes to who I am. It would be wasted if I read something that was speaking the opposite of who I am. It is not wasted if I read a good book that doesn't pull my heart away from who I am or who God is calling me to be. Some of the activities done by people who stay busy are wasted time. When you pour into something that is going to work against what you value, that is wasted time.

In stillness, you experience things in the Lord. You go places in the Lord. It doesn't mean you see angels or the throne of God necessarily. It means you are walking with the Lord on a journey. In the time of stillness with the Lord, He is taking you places. I only get to explore through activity the realms I experience in stillness. When you feel His presence, enjoy what you have; that is the key to more. When you are connected heart-to-heart and your spirit cries out "Abba Father," He is rewriting your heart to see and think differently. Then when you go to do something in ministry, you are only exploring the territory you gained in stillness.

True Greatness

True greatness only comes out of you when you are in over your head. You have to be willing to take on things you don't feel qualified for. Feeling called is way overrated. I have yet to be called into the ministry. Until then, I will be faithful with what I've been given. Some things are done just because there is a need. The Good Samaritan may not have felt called or gifted. There was a need. There is greatness in you—the grace of God, the greatness of God that is the answer to a need.

You have faithfully put yourselves in an environment where the Word of God is given daily. In the next 10 or so years, you will discover what has been put in you. It will take that long. Measure your success not by the immediate impact on a place, but that you are there. The success of fellowship is that you have brought the presence of God and shown love to the person, not that something has happened.

Keep your goals and ambitions simple. As long as, at the end of the day, you can say, "I did what He said to do," that's what matters. Maybe 10 years from now I would do it differently, but I did it the best I knew how to do today. That's a wonderful way to live because then you don't measure your success by how many people are sitting in the pew, the offering, the number of healings, how many received a prophetic word or how many are on the outreach team. We all have a spot to fill in life. It's a pretty big deal that you have these priorities sorted out because it's really easy to measure success by attendance—especially for a pastor.

You will be in different areas of responsibility, so there will be different measurements for you. Don't let the Wall Street approach to things determine whether or not you are successful. There are some pretty amazing and successful people in ministry all over the planet who have very small ministries by typical standards. It's too easy to get discouraged. If you compare yourself with people, you'll compare yourself with people less great than you, and you'll become proud. Or you'll compare yourself with people greater than you, and you'll become inferior. And neither is good. So just don't compare yourself with others. Just do what He says to do. Make it your joy to do His will. That's what Jesus did: *"My food is to do the will of Him who sent me"* (John 4:34 ESV).

You've said yes to God. Now just go back and see Him move. You don't know how burning you are in the eyes of others. What you carry is seen, and you can't measure its effect. You are not aware of what people see on you. You are in communion with the Lord. Live with the confidence that you've been chosen to carry His presence.

Celebrate the Simple

Celebrate the simple. If you can't, you'll be in trouble because you'll need the artificial to keep satisfied. Celebrate the evening with a friend. What if some of your greatest treasure was the fact that you get to sit down with a friend over cheese and crackers? Your ability to celebrate the simple says a lot about the depth within you.

When Paul was giving instructions to Timothy, he said, *"I exhort...that we may lead a quiet and peaceable life"* (1 Tim. 2:2). The target for us is not 24/7 activity, broken by just enough sleep to make it. The target is the quiet and peaceable life. If you can celebrate simplicity, God can trust you with the complex because you won't be impressed by it.

Realize that if you accomplish everything you desired, but you are uncomfortable being alone, you have missed something. If you are not happy being with yourself, that is not good. You have to be able to be comfortable within your own skin when you are alone.

I'm thankful that I get to see what was always in history, but never in my day, but I'm fighting for simplicity because simplicity is what life is made of. If at the end of your life, you have a few really, really good friends, then you have ended well.

ABOUT THE AUTHORS

You may contact any of these authors at:

Bethel Church
933 College View Dr.
Redding, CA 96003
530-246-6000
www.ibethel.org

Sheri Downs

Sheri Downs is the mother of two amazing children, Christi and Michael, and has four incredible granddaughters. Part of the Bethel family for over 20 years, Sheri expresses her mother's heart and passion for intimacy and connection in every aspect of her role as a pastor in the first-year program of Bethel School of Supernatural Ministry (BSSM).

She is available for speaking and also enjoys releasing the love of Papa through worship in prophetic song.

Joaquin Evans

Joaquin lives with his wife Renée in Redding, California, where he is the co-director of Bethel Movement Activation Teams and the previous director of the Bethel Healing Rooms. Joaquin's heart is to steward the presence of God well, and he knows that one "love encounter" can change us all. Joaquin teaches around the world, releasing and activating people in a culture of healing and revival. His passion is to develop teams that see God move in miracles, signs, and wonders so that God is displayed in love and power and Jesus gets His full reward.

Chris Gore

Chris Gore is director of Bethel's Healing Rooms. His passion is to see the Church walk in a kingdom mindset and see the saints equipped to walk in extraordinary exploits by releasing the kingdom through healings and miracles. His heart is to see churches, cities, and nations transformed.

Bill Johnson

Bill Johnson is a fifth-generation pastor with a rich heritage in the Holy Spirit. Bill and his wife, Beni, serve a growing number of churches through a leadership network that crosses denominational lines and builds relationships. The Johnsons are the senior pastors of Bethel Church in Redding, California. All three of their children and spouses are involved in full-time ministry. They have eight wonderful grandchildren.

Paul Manwaring

Paul Manwaring is on the Senior Leadership Team at Bethel Church, Redding, California and oversees Global Legacy: Bethel's apostolic relational network. He passionately pursues the manifestation of God's glory on the earth, the transformation of lives and organizations, and the erasure of the secular/sacred dividing line. Paul spent 19 years in senior prison management in England, is a Registered General and Psychiatric Nurse, and holds an MSt in management from Cambridge University.

Stefanie Overstreet

Stefanie Overstreet is a registered nurse specializing in pediatrics and maternity. She loves traveling and ministering with her husband and is passionate about medical missions focused on underprivileged children worldwide—especially those in Africa. Stefanie and her husband Chris, the outreach pastor at Bethel Church, live in Redding, California.

Pam Spinosi

Pam Spinosi serves Bethel Church in two roles: testimony writer and international student liaison for BSSM. A college ESL and English instructor by profession, she teaches writing classes at BSSM, edits books and documents, and presents at Bethel's Writing Unto the Glory Conference, which she launched and has organized four times since 2006.

Deborah Sawka Stevens

Deborah Sawka Stevens was born in Canada and moved to Redding in 2002. Upon graduating from BSSM, she was hired to develop the Media and Events Department. Deborah is passionate about seeing people go deeper in their relationship with God and with one another through continual encounters with the tangible love, fire, and glory of God.

Crystal Stiles

Crystal Stiles is a pastor and associate overseer in Bethel School of Supernatural Ministry. She has a passion to walk as a friend of God and help others come into greater intimacy with Him. She has been a part of the Bethel family for the past seven years.

In the right hands, This Book will Change Lives!

Most of the people who need this message will not be looking for this book. To change their lives, you need to put a copy of this book in their hands.

> *But others (seeds) fell into good ground, and brought forth fruit, some a hundred-fold, some sixty-fold, some thirty-fold* (Matthew 13:8).

Our ministry is constantly seeking methods to find the good ground, the people who need this anointed message to change their lives. Will you help us reach these people?

> *Remember this—a farmer who plants only a few seeds will get a small crop. But the one who plants generously will get a generous crop* (2 Corinthians 9:6).

EXTEND THIS MINISTRY BY SOWING
3 BOOKS, 5 BOOKS, 10 BOOKS, OR MORE TODAY,
AND BECOME A LIFE CHANGER!

Thank you,

Don Nori Sr., Founder
Destiny Image
Since 1982